$7.50

Westward to Alki

Old Denny School, located on the original David Denny claim.

Westward to Alki

The Story of David and Louisa Denny

By Gordon Newell

A Seattle Historical Society Publication
through a research grant provided by
Victor W.S. Denny, Jr.

Photographs from the Museum of History and Industry Collection, Seattle Historical Society, Seattle, Washington.

Superior PUBLISHING COMPANY

COPYRIGHT 1977 by Superior Publishing Company

Seattle, Washington

All Rights Reserved

Library of Congress Cataloging in Publication Data

Newell, Gordon R.
  Westward to Alki.

  Includes index.
  1. Denny, David. 2. Denny, Louisa.
3. Seattle—Biography. 4. Frontier and pioneer life—Washington (State)—Seattle.
I. Title.
F899.S453D466   979.7'77 [B]   76-56785
ISBN 0-87564-807-X

First Edition

Printed in the United States of America

CONTENTS

I	Foreword, Victor W.S. Denny Jr. .	1
II	Introduction: Smaquamox	4
III	Londonderry to the Shenandoah .	6
IV	From the Shenandoah to the Mississippi	10
V	From the Mississippi to the Platte	14
VI	From the Platte to the Columbia .	19
VIII	From the Columbia to Puget Sound	25
IX	New York Alki	40
X	Timber and Muscle	49
XI	Sweetbriar Bride	59
XII	Indian War	65
XIII	Aftermath	81
XIV	The Later Years	94
XV	Epilogue: Return to the Wilderness	109
XVI	Index	121

Le Daneys

Denny

QUARTERED COAT OF ARMS USED BY SIR ANTHONY DENNY AND HIS SUCCESSORS IN SUBSTITUTION OF THE ANCIENT DENNY ARMS.

Coats of Arms of various branches of the Denny family.

FOREWORD

My good friend H. W. McCurdy has often quoted to me the words of Macaulay... *"People who take no pride in the noble achievements of remote ancestors, will never achieve anything worthy to be remembered with pride by remote descendants"* ... while urging me to have recorded the story of my grandparents, David and Louisa Denny.

I have decided to do so because I believe that story has not been fully told by past historians, and because I do "take pride in the noble achievements" of these not so remote ancestors.

As a matter of fact, my grandmother, Louisa Boren Denny, was an alert and vital woman well into my teen-age years, and as a boy I often listened spellbound to her personal reminiscences of the landing at Alki, the Battle of Seattle, and the details of pioneer life in the then primitive and isolated Northwest frontier. I remember particularly her repeating to me from memory the moving oration of Chief Seattle which he delivered in his native tongue at the signing of the Point Elliott Treaty, and her conviction that his noble words, delivered in his native tongue, had indeed been translated accurately.

When my generation is gone, people and events of pioneer days on Puget Sound will, in fact, become remote chapters in history books, for there will be no one left who knew and talked to those who lived and made that history.

This, then, is the story of David Denny, who was, quite literally, Seattle's first citizen, and of his "sweetbriar bride", Louisa.

It is a story they were certainly too busy, and I think too modest, to write themselves.

Victor W.S. Denny, Jr.
Seattle, Washington

"Every part of this country is sacred to my people. Every hillside, every valley, every plain and grove has been hallowed by some fond memory or some sad experience of my tribe. Even the rocks, which seem to lie dumb as they swelter in the sun along the silent sea shore in solemn grandeur thrill with memories of past events connected with the lives of my people; the very dust under your feet responds more lovingly to our footsteps than to yours, because it is the ashes of our ancestors, and our bare feet are conscious of the sympathetic touch, for the soil is rich with the life of our kindred.

"The noble braves, fond mothers, glad, happy-hearted maidens, and even the little children, who lived and rejoiced here for a brief season, and whose very names are not forgotten, still love these sombre solitudes, and their deep fastnesses which at eventide grow shadowy with the presence of dusky spirits.

"When the Red Man shall have perished from this earth and the memory of my tribe shall have become a myth among the White Men these shores will swarm with the invisible dead of my tribe and when your children's children think themselves alone in the field, the store, the shop, upon the highway, or in the silence of the pathless woods, they will not be alone. In all the earth there is no place dedicated to solitude. At night when the streets of your cities and villages are silent and you think them deserted, they will throng with the returning hosts that once filled and still love this beautiful land. The White Man will never be alone."

"Let him be just and deal kindly with my people, for the dead are not powerless.

"Dead—did I say? There is no death. Only a change of worlds!"

. . . *closing words of Chief Seattle's oration*
  Point Elliott treaty grounds
  January 23, 1855

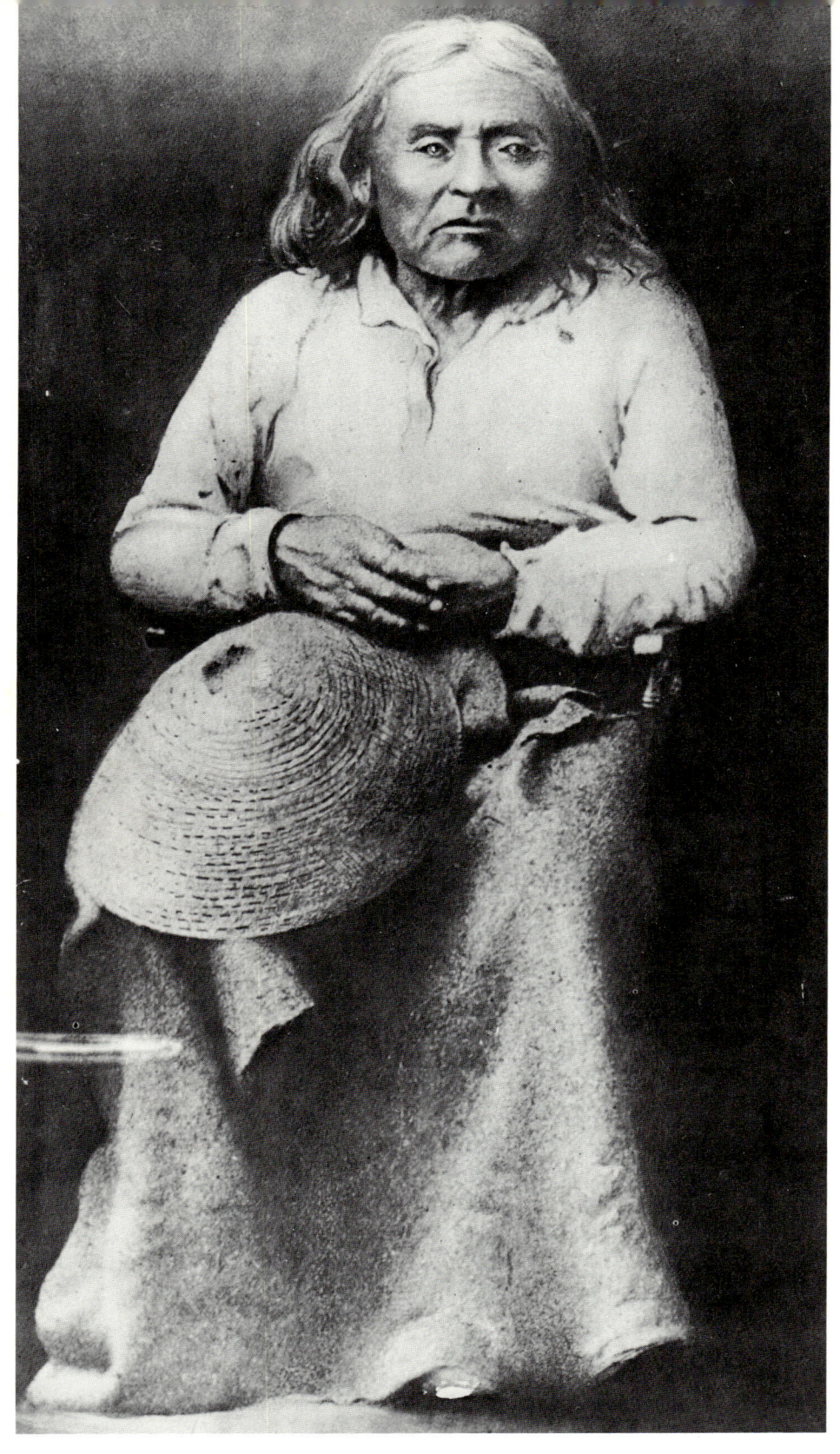

Only known photograph of Chief Seattle.

INTRODUCTION

Smaquamox

The empty bay, its five miles of curving shoreline backed by seven hills crowned with a centuries-old jungle of towering evergreen trees and shoulder-high undergrowth, appeared devoid of all human life. The only movement was the restless tossing of the giant trees and the surge of salt water on the beach below; the only sound the moaning of the autumn wind and the hiss of the cold deluge of rain sweeping in before it from the vast reaches of the Pacific Ocean.

It was the evening of November 12, 1851, and the place was Elliott Bay, so named ten years before in honor of Chaplain J. L. Elliott of the United States Navy exploration party led by Lieutenant Charles Wilkes to make the first American survey of Puget Sound. In the summer of 1841 Wilkes' cartographers had drawn a beautiful and remarkably accurate chart of the wilderness harbor, but the explorers were not impressed with its future potential and did not include it among the possible sites for commercial development.

Even before the arrival of the Wilkes party, in 1833, Dr. William Tolmie, chief factor on Puget Sound for the Hudson's Bay Company, had scouted the area as a possible site for a trading post, but rejected it because of "an unproductive soil" and "the inconvenience of going at least one-half mile for a supply of water". Tolmie was referring to the only shorelands that weren't covered with an impenetrable forest . . . the low and sandy peninsula at the southern entrance of the bay called "Smaquamox" by the Duwamish and Suquamish Indians, and now known as Alki Point. Tolmie had described it thus in his journal:

"*It is about a mile in length and from one hundred to one hundred and fifty yards in extent, raised about thirty feet above sea level, toward which it presented a steep, clayey bank. Surface flat and dotted with small pines, but soil composed almost entirely of sand. . . At its northern extremity the coast is indented with a bay five or six miles wide, and perhaps three long, into which a river flows . . . the south side of bay and river is inhabited by Tuamish Indians, of whom we saw several parties along the coast, miserably poor and destitute of fire arms.*"

Eighteen years later the "Tuamish"* Indians still camped occasionally on the peninsula they called Smaquamox and lonely Elliott Bay seemingly unchanged, with darkness already shrouding the trackless forest to the east and night coming down with the November rain along the beach to merge with the luminous haze of Indian campfires. From the lighthouse off Cape Flattery in the open Pacific 120 miles to the northwest, and the candle-lit windows of Olympia, a village of 150 white settlers at the head of Puget Sound 57 miles to the south, no sail or running lights of any ship marked the dark, wind-whipped waters of the Inland Sea.

But change had come to Elliott Bay and it would never be the same again, for out on the low-shored and lightly-timbered peninsula of Smaquamox was the beginning of a city with a white population of one . . . a youth of nineteen, wounded, sick, hungry and huddled, Indian style, in a wet blanket in the embryonic city's only building . . . a log cabin without a roof.

---

*White settlers had difficulty in adapting the gutteral speech of the Northwest Indians to written form, and Dr. Tolmie was no exception. The general accepted spelling of his "Tuamish" has become Duwamish. Tolmie referred to the affiliated Suquamish tribe as the "So-quo-mish" and to Chief Seattle or Sealth of the confederated tribes as "See-alt".

Remains of the original log cabin at Alki Point, 1893.

The single white resident of the future city of Seattle had crossed the plains that year from Illinois and for three weeks he had been alone in the sombre solitude, except for visits from the Indians. A few days before, while working on the unfinished cabin, he had slashed his foot to the bone with an ax and the wound had left him unable to work or hunt for food. He was shaking with malarial chills and fever and his jaws ached with the agony of neuralgia. That afternoon, hobbling back on an improvised crutch from an inspection of the future townsite, he had found a family of skunks in possession of his doubtful shelter.

Having survived the crossing of the plains and mountains by prairie schooner and a 200-mile hike through the howling wilderness from the Columbia River to Elliott Bay, the teen-aged pioneer was no fool. He waited patiently in the rain until the skunks had consumed the last of his food and departed. The only remaining amenities were an improvised and leaky shelter of fir boughs, a small package of tea that the skunks had spurned and the unconquerable spirit of a boy of nineteen named David Thomas Denny.

CHAPTER ONE

Londonderry to the Shenandoah

The arrival of David Denny on America's last frontier marked the culmination of westward migration by many generations of his family over centuries of time and ten thousand miles of land and sea. A restless urge to explore new lands and build new homes in the wilderness had been in the Denny blood from the dim beginnings of recorded history.

Surviving records of the time indicate that members of the Denny family were with William of Normandy in 1066 when he conquered England and its Saxon defenders, but it seems likely that the family's beginnings were in the runic pre-history of the Viking sea wanderers. In Normandy the French spelling of the name was *le Daney* or *le Deney*, literally "the Dane", derived, genealogists believe, from Bernard the Dane, the Danish prince who, with his brother Rollo, conquered Normandy and whose descendants moved westward again across the English Channel in the eleventh century.

The first written records of a member of the Denny family in England refer to Geoffrey Denny, born about 1329 and later listed as "Patron of the Living" of the Church of All Hallows Staining, believed to have been the first stone church in London. Geoffrey appears to have been ancestor of kinsman of most branches of the Denny family.

In subsequent years the family settled throughout England and its branches extended to Scotland. The ancient town of Denny near Dumbarton probably took its name from one of these early settlers of the Denny family. Gilmori de Deny (William of Denny), a Baille of Dumbarton, was one of the first to appear in the written records of Scotland. It was his descendants who formed the famous Dumbarton shipbuilding firm of William Denny and Brothers.

Others felt the recurring call of the Viking wanderlust and migrated again, this time from Greenloch and Dumbarton to the northern Irish county of Ulster.

It was one of these "Ulster Scots", David Denny, Sr., the great grandfather of young David Thomas Denny who, in the late 1730's, continued the family migration that began in Denmark in the dark ages and ended at last, in 1851, on the shores of Puget Sound.

In the three-volume *Denny Genealogy* by Margaret Collins Denny Dixon and Elizabeth Chapman Denny Vann, the origin of the Ulster Scots and the forces which shaped their character are described as follows:

"*For centuries the English Crown had striven to subdue the turbulent Celtic Irish people. Following the Irish revolt in the time of Queen Elizabeth, more and more emphasis was placed on the settlement in Ireland of Englishmen who would be attached to the Crown, and who might help in bringing the Irish to acquiescence in English rule. Francis Bacon was advocating these 'plantations' in 1606 and the title of Baronet was created in 1611, to be granted to English gentry who would emigrate to Ireland.*

"*After various Irish insurrections, about two million acres in the north of Ireland, almost the whole of the six northern counties, came into the possession of the Crown by 'the* ancient Roman policy' of confiscation. Since landholding was a personal relationship between king and liege, it was customary to give Crown lands to those who were loyal. Thus, when James VI of Scotland came to the throne of England as James I, it was judged that further 'plantations' would be a solution for the troublesome 'Irish Question'. This was at first planned solely for the English, but it was natural for the Scottish friends of the king to wish to share in his bounty, and about 1610 the Irish land was also opened to certain Scotsmen, who might arrange to bring over Scottish settlers to Northern Ireland. These Scots came mostly from the Lowlands and were almost as English as if they had come from the North of England. While the treatment of the Irish is said to have been less severe than the treatment of disloyal persons in Scotland, yet it was an 'iron age' and men from the 'Border' of England and Scotland would have few scruples in subduing troublesome neighbors, it was hoped. For a variety of reasons large numbers of Scottish immigrants were found and for many years they poured across the Irish Sea to the 'free land' offered them in Ireland."

But, as the *Genealogy* points out, life in Ireland proved to be no bed of roses for the Ulster Scots. Within a few years the hostility of the displaced Irish was matched by that of the English monarchy:

"By the time Charles I came to the throne in 1625, religious difficulties between the Irish Catholics and the Presbyterian invaders was well developed. Furthermore, Charles I believed in the absolute authority of the Crown. The independent Scots in Ireland were opposed to absolutism in government, were dissenters from the established English Church, and naturally fell back on their difference in religion as one means of expressing this opposition. This brought forth retaliatory measures from the English government. So, as early as 1636, Scottish clergymen, who had been deposed from their chapels in Ireland, sailed for America with their flocks in the Eagle Wing, but were driven back by storms. All this religious disturbance was little help toward the king's plans for securing the submission and conformity of the Irish.

"In October, 1641, there was a sudden rebellion of the oppressed Irish and they took this occasion to slaughter a great number of the unwelcome Presbyterian foreigners who had settled on their lands. The number killed has been reported to be as low as eight thousand and as high as two-hundred thousand, depending on the bias of the person doing the reporting. Naturally the armies of the king punished this rebellion with equal ferocity, but the king exerted himself to bring the hostilities to an end. This civil war lasted from 1641 to 1653.

"Not many Scots came into Ireland in the next few years, and the 'type' of character which came to be known as the 'Ulster Scot' began to be fixed at this time. By 1660, a state document said: 'There are 40,000 Irish and 80,000 Scots in Ulster ready to bear arms', this in spite of the fact that, after the 1641 massacres, many returned to Scotland and others had turned to the New World for refuge.

"With the restoration of Charles II to the throne, immediate proceedings were taken by Parliament against Non-Conformists, and the Presbyterian Church in Ulster was an early target. These harsh laws caused further migration between 1660-1665, and this continued under his successor, James II.

"When the English Revolution of 1688 began, the Irish Catholics rose in support of James II. Many Presbyterians who opposed William and Mary emigrated to America at that time. Ulster Presbyterians who declared allegiance to William and Mary, claimants to the throne, remained in Ireland. Then came the famous Londonderry siege, lasting one hundred and five days, and the final overthrow of the Jacobites.

"But, even though they had supported the claim of William and Mary to the throne, the fact that the Ulster Scots were Dissenters from the Church of England brought immediate severe measures upon them. They were prohibited from holding public office and being married by their own ministers (which was not legalized until 1737). Their chapels were closed, they were not allowed to hold schools for their children. They must be buried by the established church. They had become virtual outlaws. Dean Swift said the people were in worse condition than the peasants of France or the vassals in Germany and Poland.

"Their economic condition had become extremely bad. They had brought with them from Scotland their sheep culture and the *weaving of woolen cloth, but laws of 1698 forbade the exportation of woolens, save to England and Wales, which ruined the woolen trade. Instead, the manufacture of linen, in which they were not skilled, was decreed. Many were driven from their farms at the expiration of their leases. From 1714 to 1719 there was insufficient rainfall, the flax failed, the sheep died. In 1716 there were severe frosts and in 1718 smallpox ravaged the section. Their high taxes were ruinous. A sympathetic investigator, Archbishop King, reported: 'I cannot see how any more can be got from them except we take away their potatoes and butter-milk or flay them and sell their skins'. Farming was discouraged by the English landlords in favor of sheep grazing. There was insufficient imported food and hundreds died of famine. Even so, they considered the restrictions on religion a heavier burden. 'They were willing to starve peacefully but not to be thwarted in their views of right and heaven'.*

"With the accession of George I in 1714 the real ferment for emigration appeared and 'went through Ulster like a fever'. Many persons came to America in 1716. Five or six hundred came between 1718 and 1720. Six thousand came in 1720. In 1729 six crowded vessels arrived in Philadelphia in one week. The great migration continued to 1750, until a third of the population of Ulster had departed. One man wrote from America: 'I am of the opinion that all the north of Ireland will be over here in a little time.'"

According to the most reliable sources, David Denny, Sr., remained stubbornly on the family land near Londonderry until the late 1730's. Having done everything possible to make conditions unbearable for the Ulster Scots, the authorities had, by that time, taken further measures to discourage their seeking new lives in the New World. When the Irish Parliament tried to pass a measure banning migration, "it only stimulated departures."

The "Landlords and Tythers", who were profiting from the deprivations of the Ulster Scot tenants, persecuted shipowners and master mariners engaged in the emigrant trade, as well as printers who produced advertisements for overseas colonists. One man who threatened to whip any such advertiser was cautioned by a judge that "It must be done according to law."

Glowing reports from America were officially denied, but the long land leases given to the Scots in North Ireland were expiring, and could only be renewed at ruinous cost. The knowledge that one could have fertile land and religious liberty in America could not be suppressed and David Denny finally joined the great exodus.

One of his granddaughters (Isabella Denny Hubbard), when a very old woman, recalled that David had left Ireland on account of the "great derth", and that he had paid the passage of poorer neighbors. This first "Denny party" of American pioneers landed in Pennsylvania and settled there among the other Ulster Scots who, according to the *Denny Genealogy*, "had been established by the Proprietors beyond the Quaker settlements on the seaboard as a buffer against the Indians".

History was repeating itself, as it would continue to do in the saga of the descendants of old David Denny in America. Just as the first Ulster Scots were granted lands in North Ireland in the days of James I as a shield against the rebellious Irish, so those of a century later . . . tougher, hardier and more independent than the Quakers and German Mennonites, Amish, Dunkers and Moravians who had later migrated to Pennsylvania in search of religious freedom . . . were encouraged to establish a new frontier in the Cumberland Valley and southwestern Pennsylvania.

Such was the sturdy stock of which George Washington said that if the Revolution were lost and he had but one banner left, he would rally his Scotch-Irish troopers and plant a new Republic on top of the Blue Ridge Mountains.

Although family records of this period are incomplete and frequently conflicting, it appears that David Denny, soon after his arrival in America, joined the Ulster Scots pioneers on the frontier in Lancaster County, where records indicate that he was living in 1744. It was there that he married a Margaret Denny, possibly a distant cousin, and that the first of their seven children was born, probably in 1741.

Here it was, too, that the family had its first, but certainly not its last, encounter, with Indian hostility, the *Denny Genealogy* recording:

"Their peaceful existence was rudely shattered when John Armstrong, a trader, and his two servants, were murdered by a Delaware Indian. Such an event was a threat to every settler's home. A posse was organized, the bodies were found and buried. The murderer was brought in and imprisoned at 'Lancaster'. On April 19, 1744, David Denny was one of nine men who signed a deposition setting forth the facts of the search and capture".

The growing family later pushed on to the Brandywine neighborhood of Chester County, where records of 1757 indicate that David Denny was a member of the crew of a "Battoe, hired in ye service of ye prov'ce of Pennsylvania."*

Thereafter the name of David Denny, Sr., disappears from the records of Pennsylvania and it appears that the restless pioneer was smitten by the "Virginia Fever" . . . the pre-Revolutionary equivalent of the "Oregon Fever" that would, a century later, send his grandson and great grandsons half way across a continent to the last frontier.

The Blue Ridge Mountains had been an effective barrier to western expansion during the first hundred years of colonial settlement, but now a way to the Shenandoah Valley had been opened from the Cumberland Valley of Pennsylvania. David and Margaret Denny and their seven children joined the migration across the Blue Ridge in 1764, traveling as would the later pioneers, by covered wagon. In March of that year David had bought 194 acres of land in the newly settled Frederick County from one William Hoge, for which he paid "100 pounds current money" and, two months later, an additional 235 acres "near Round Hill on the Draughts of Hoge Creek" from Isaac Greenleafe.

It was on those lands that the sturdy old Ulster Scots pioneer died in the summer of 1777. His will and inventory of estate provide an interesting insight into the material accomplishments of his forty-odd years as a frontiersman in the New World and the social customs of his era.

He left his "well Beloved" wife, Margaret, a life interest in his dwelling house and garden. Since household furniture commonly belonged to the husband, even the wife's own spinning wheel was listed in the will as a bequest to her, as was "the bed on which we usually lay", and a chest. He also left Margaret "one bake pan, one of the four stew pots and all the pewter and earthenware". The rest of his personal estate went to his fifth son, Robert, who was to pay his mother 10 pounds a year, as well as "provide food, fuel and care in sickness".

No tables or chairs were listed in the household inventory, but there was a "liberry" of books, complete with book case. There were a few farming tools, but a high value was placed on his blacksmith's "belles" (bellows) and other iron and wood working implements. The "waggon of cloth", (the Conestoga wagon that had carried the family and their goods from Pennsylvania), with horses and harness, was valued at 102 pounds. By custom, the homestead was left to the two youngest sons, Robert and Samuel. Two cows each were left to his sons, William John and Samuel.

As the hard-earned fruits of nearly half a century in the New World, David Denny left behind him considerable property, a daughter, six sturdy sons, numerous grandchildren . . . and a pioneering heritage that would lead his descendants across the plains and mountains to found a new city and a new frontier.

---

*Pennsylvania Archives, 5th Series, Vol. 1, p. 100

CHAPTER TWO

From the Shenandoah to the Mississippi

Robert Denny, fifth son of David, was born during the family's stay in Pennsylvania . . . in 1753 . . . and was a boy of eleven during the journey through the Blue Ridge Mountains to the Shenandoah Valley. It appears that his father, the possessor of that rare frontier "liberry" of books, saw to it that his son received at least the rudiments of a formal education.

The year after his father's death, in May of 1778, Robert married 20-year-old Rachel Thomas and, less than a year later, enlisted in the Revolutionary Army as a private, serving successively as quartermaster sergeant, ensign, paymaster and lieutenant. At one time, it is recorded in the *Denny Genealogy*, "he was given the painful duty of raiding the gun shop of his eldest brother Walter", who had married the daughter of a wealthy Virginia family and become an avowed Tory. On another occasion he was placed in charge of Hessian prisoners of war captured at "Little York". Legend has it that when Lord Fairfax, who held large estates in the Shenandoah Valley and was an ardent Tory, saw so many Hessian soldiers marching toward Lieutenant Denny's stockade, he became convinced that the English had won the war, and suffered an apoplectic stroke when he learned the true state of affairs.

After the war and following the death of his mother, with whose care he had been charged, Robert Denny was free to follow the seemingly inborn family urge to move westward. This he did in 1787, setting out with his wife and three small sons for Kentucky, possibly in the Conestoga wagon that had brought the family from Pennsylvania 23 years earlier. They settled in Lincoln County, where the former revolutionary army officer "secured at least 333 acres on Shawnee Run". Within the next few years he was followed by three of his brothers, William and Samuel, who had also been officers in the Army of the newly-formed United States, and John, a surveyor.

Over the years Robert and Rachel became the parents of seven sons and two daughters, all imbued with the stern Presbyterian moral code of their Ulster Scots ancestors. As the sons of Robert Denny grew up and were married, slavery grew increasingly distasteful to them and, one by one, the third generation families packed their goods and chattels and moved across the Ohio River to the free Territory of Indiana.

In November, 1808, Robert Denny's wife of 30 years died and was buried at Shawnee Run Baptist Church. There was nothing to keep him longer in Kentucky and he set about to sell his property there. By 1813, at the age of

10

sixty, he had wound up his affairs and, with his unmarried daughter Sarah, set out on horseback for Indiana Territory. They traveled by easy stages, stopping at frontier taverns along the way for overnight lodging. Robert carried the gold coins he had received for his Kentucky lands in his saddlebags, putting them every night for safekeeping in the room where he slept. One morning when he checked the bags he found them filled with stones instead of gold. The thief had left him destitute and he never fully recovered from the blow. He died in 1826 at the age of 73 at the home of his eldest son, where he had lived most of the remainder of his life.

Of Robert Denny's nine children it was the sixth, John Denny, who would lead the family on its final migration to the ultimate western outpost of American civilization.

Born May 4, 1793, on his father's Kentucky farm, John Denny was the epitome of the American pioneer and frontiersman; citizen soldier and homespun politican. Just as his father and uncles had volunteered for service in the Revolutionary War, John enlisted for the War of 1812 in the Kentucky Mounted Volunteers at the age of 19. As a sergeant of cavalry, he was present at the death of the legendary Indian chief, Tecumseh, and at the Battle of the Thames in Canada he was run over by a herd of stampeding horses. He suffered a broken knee that never mended properly and thereafter was handicapped by a "game leg", which probably caused him some discomfort, but certainly didn't slow him down appreciably. During the course of a long and colorful life he helped in the settlement and development of five states.

According to his own account, his experience as a teen-aged trooper in the War of 1812 taught him the evils of drink and made him a lifelong teetotaler. A half century later in Seattle he described the conversion as follows to a friend and fellow Washington Territory politician, L. B. Andrews:

"When I was a soldier in the War of 1812 we captured some British stores on the Maumee River, and among them were some kegs of liquor. The boys got to sampling them, I along the rest, and before I knew it the tarnal stuff had got my legs tied up into double bowknots, and how they ever straightened out again I don't know to this day, but I do know that I lay in the guard house for three days afterward, and when I came out I felt the way a dog would that had been caught stealing sheep. Boys, don't you ever tackle 'old alcohol' for a wrastle, for he's sure to get the under holts and'll throw you every time".

After his discharge from the Mounted Volunteers in 1814 young John Denny married 17-year-old Sarah Wilson in Kentucky, but within the year they were on their way to join his brothers in Washington County, Indiana Territory. There he had his first experience with the malarial fever that was to afflict the family for the next 35 years or more, or, as he picturesquely put it, "We had many a wrastle with the ague there".

He put up with the discomforts of periodic chills and fever for eight years, but in 1823 he moved his family on to Putnam County, Indiana, which was then an undeveloped wilderness. There he hewed out a farm from the beech woods and built a cabin for his wife Sarah and four small sons, ranging in age from eight-year-old Lewis to one-year-old Arthur Armstrong Denny.

By 1834 the "ague" and civilization had caught up with John Denny again. He sold his land, packed his goods and family, which then included eight sons, and again took up the westward march to Knox County, Illinois, which was close enough to the frontier of civilization to give him "elbow room" for the next 16 years.

At the time of the family's arrival in Illinois the four eldest sons were of an age to help their father build and work the new farm in what became the placid rural community of Cherry Grove. Lewis was 19, Alford 17, John Fletcher 15, and Arthur 12. Even ten-year-old James and seven-year-old Samuel, in the tradition of the American frontier, were expected to pitch in and perform their assigned chores. Only two-year old David Thomas and his year-old brother A.W. (Wiley) were too small to lend a hand laying out the new fields and building the new home.

By 1841 the Illinois homestead had, by the standards of the times, become a prosperous and comfortable home. Some of the amenities of advancing civilization had come to the former frontier community, including a log cabin "subscription" school two miles or so from the Denny farm, where the boys received the "book larnin'" insisted upon by their father.

It was in 1841 that Sarah Denny, John's wife of 27 years, died at the age of 44. Her first grandchild, whom she had looked forward to since the marriage of her third son, John, was not born until three months after her death.

In the autumn of 1848, at the hale and hearty age of 55, John Denny married another Sarah . . . Sarah Latimer Boren, the widow of a Tennessee Baptist minister who had died a few years after her marriage, leaving her with three small children. After migrating to Illinois with her father, she had moved to Cherry Grove, bought a log cabin and established a home for her children. John Denny, who was by this time a man of substance in his community, was no doubt impressed with the independent character and pioneer spirit of the attractive middle-aged widow and the match proved a happy one for both of them.

Although he frequently alluded to his lack of "book larnin'", John Denny was an avid reader, his keen mind was a storehouse of facts, and he was possessed of the kind of earthy humor and rare story-telling ability that had carried Abraham Lincoln to the White House.

As a matter of fact, John Denny and Abe Lincoln became close friends and political allies during their years in Illinois, for they had much in common. There was even some physical resemblance between the two, although Denny was 16 years older than Lincoln and, at five feet, ten inches, a good half-foot shorter than the rangy rail-splitter, a tintype portrait taken of him in middle age is remarkably Lincolnesque in almost every facial detail, including the fringe of chin whiskers that became a Lincoln trademark.

The ready wit and keen sense of humor, which it was said made his presence a "mirth provoking contagion", no doubt helped endear John Denny to Abraham Lincoln, as did his firm loyalty to the Whig party. Certainly the most delightful anecdote regarding their personal and political association was one first published by his friend L. B. Andrews in the Seattle *Intelligencer* in territorial days:

"In early days Uncle John had been a 'whig' and in 'Illinoi' had fought many a hard battle with the common enemy. He had represented his district repeatedly in the legislature of that state, and he used to tell with pride and a good deal of satisfaction how one day a little handful of whigs, Old Abe and himself among the number, broke up a quorum of the house by jumping from a second story window of the statehouse at Springfield, thereby preventing the passage of a bill by the democrats which was obnoxious to the whigs. The democrats had been watching their opportunity, and having secured a quorum with but a few whigs in the house, locked the doors and proposed to put their measure through. But the whigs, led by Old Abe and Uncle John, nipped the little game in the manner related".

Had John Denny chosen to remain active in Illinois politics he might have moved with Abraham Lincoln to the national capital. Instead, he moved westward again.

By 1850, with Lincoln defeated for reelection after a single term in Congress, and apparently sinking into political oblivion, the "Oregon Fever" was sweeping Illinois along with the rest of the nation. Roberta Frye Watt, a great granddaughter of John Denny, wrote of those days in her book *Four Wagons West**:

"Mother's earliest recollections went back to her old family home in the little town of Cherry Grove, Illinois. She remembered the family gathered around the fireside on winter evenings while her father (Arthur Denny) read letters from Farley Pierce, Liberty Wallace and other venturesome souls who had gone out to Oregon to seek their fortunes; she remembered when the neighbors dropped in and discussed the news from their friends. The letters told of the wonders of the Pacific; the grandeur of the mountains; the vastness of the untouched forests; but best of all they told of the mild climate and fertile soil and of the flowers that blossom in the winter time.

"Magic words and magic letters from a magic land, they seemed to her childish mind as she sat before the fire and toasted her little toes. Many times the letters were read; then folded and put away. Then came one evening colder than usual. Grandfather had plodded home through a snow storm and after supper he took out the letters and read them again. Still holding them in his hand, he went to the window, pulled the curtain aside and looked out, then turning to Grandmother, he asked, 'Mary, will you go?'

"And Grandmother answered . . . 'Yes, Arthur'.

"And so was the great decision made.

"When Grandfather told his father and brothers that he and Grandmother had decid-

---
*Four Wagons West; The Story of Seattle, Binfords & Mort, Publishers, Portland, Oregon, 1931.

ed to go to Oregon, it was like a final word they had been waiting to receive".

Emily Inez Denny, daughter of David and great granddaughter of John, in her earlier book, *Blazing the Way**, agreed that the letters from former neighbors had a strong influence on the family, as did "the perusal of Fremont's travels" and "the desire for a change of climate from the rigorous one of Illinois" and, no doubt most importantly, "the possession of a pioneering spirit". But she wrote that it was the family patriarch, John Denny, who "was the leading spirit".

Just which Denny it was that made the momentous decision remains unknown. It seems likely that most of this family of pioneers had a hopeless case of Oregon Fever by 1850 and that it took little urging to set them to packing the covered wagons again. The fact that "Uncle John" was rounding out 57 hard years of frontier life and had achieved a comfortable and respected place in the community certainly didn't slow *him* down. After all, his father had pulled up stakes and ridden horseback from Kentucky to Indiana at the age of 60.

Arthur Denny, a no-nonsense individual who had failed to inherit his father's superb sense of humor, wasted no time in explaining his motivation in moving west when he wrote his crusty reminiscences of pioneer life* 37 years after the historic trek began. He recorded bluntly, *"We left our Illinois home on April 10, 1851, and crossed Iowa from Burlington to Kanesville, a Mormon town, (now Council Bluffs) on the Missouri river, traveling via New London, Mount Pleasant, Fairfield Agency, Ottumwa and Eddyville".*

Three generations of the family planted in the New World by the old Ulster Scot, David Denny, were headed west again, their covered wagons plodding toward a final river crossing . . . that of the Columbia, the ultimate Great River of the West.

It was their intention to plant new farms in the fertile valley of the Columbia's tributary Willamette River, but destiny would lead them still further into the profound wilderness of the far Northwest where, instead of crops, they would plant the seeds of a great city.

---

*Blazing the Way, or True Stories, Songs and Sketches of Puget Sound and other Pioneers, Rainier Printing Co. Inc., Seattle, Washington, 1909.

*Pioneer Days on Puget Sound by A. A. Denny, Seattle, W. T., C. B. Bagley, Printer, 1888.

"Emigrants Crossing the Plain" by F.O.C. Darley.

CHAPTER THREE

From the Mississippi to the Platte

Arthur Denny's granddaughter Roberta provided far more details of the family exodus, including warm and human touches (which the men of the party probably hadn't noticed).

"To decide was to act. The months following were filled with busy preparations for the journey. Hams were cured; blankets were woven; warm comforters made; and the household linen replenished. The women sewed far into the night making stout garments for themselves and the children. Even the children's little fingers were kept busy carding wool and piecing quilts. The cobbler came and made shoes for the whole family. New harnesses were bought and the wagons were provided with strong, heavy springs.

"The old homes were sold. The household goods were scattered among friends and relatives, for only the things that were absolutely necessary and those that could be packed conveniently into the covered wagons were kept. Most of the provisions were crammed into sacks to save the weight of boxes.

"It was a saying in those days that nothing must be taken on the trail that was not worth a dollar a pound. I doubt that Louisa Boren was particular about the value per pound of the wall mirror that she wanted to take. Her elders objected on account of the extra weight and the risk of breakage. However, Louisa would have her way; when no one was looking she tucked it in".

At 24, Louisa Boren was petite, feminine and very pretty, but she had nothing in common with those mid-nineteenth century maidens who were expected to obediently let the menfolk do their thinking for them. She had grown up on the frontier and, like her pioneer mother, Sarah Boren Denny, she had a mind of her own and wasn't afraid to speak it when she felt it necessary . . . a characteristic that probably saved a good many lives before the journey was over.

Louisa's practicality was leavened by a sort of common-sense romanticism and sentiment. She was the only one who remembered that there would be a first Christmas in the new and lonely land for which they were bound. In addition to the mirror, she smuggled some small trinkets for the children aboard the covered wagon and kept them carefully hidden until that day came. She also carried a packet of sweetbriar seeds from Cherry Grove to be planted on the last frontier. Roberta Frye Watt explained the origin of Louisa's legendary sweetbriar seeds in her book:

"One day shortly before the emigrants started, Louisa and her dearest girlhood friend, Pamelia Dunlap, visited for the last time. As they stood together in the sweet, old-fashioned garden of Edmond Dunlap, two quaint girls of the Fifties . . . Louisa, dark and vivacious; Pamelia, fair-haired and quiet . . . there came over them the realization that they might never see each other

John Denny.

Arthur A. Denny.

again in this world. For a while their grief overwhelmed them. Louisa was the first to recover. She would take the sweetbriar seeds that she had gathered in this very garden, she said, and plant them at her new home. It was like a tryst that they were to keep, and somehow it comforted them".

And, according to her granddaughter's account, Louisa's older sister Mary Ann must have had her own share of combined sentiment and strong-mindedness, for when the wagons were loaded and the party ready to set out on their long journey she delayed things while she bade a lonely farewell to her old home . . . a waste of time that must surely have annoyed her husband, Arthur Denny, who, once he had made up his mind, made it a practice never to look back . . . particularly for the purpose of shedding sentimental tears:

"I have been told now, when the travelers were ready to start, my grandmother walked through the empty, echoing rooms of her home for the last time with a strange feeling of unreality. For months all had worked and planned for this time of departure, which was always in the future. But now the hour, the very minute had come when she must turn her back upon her old home, old scenes, old friends . . . and she was unprepared. She went from room to room . . . out into the kitchen where she had spent so many busy hours. But there was no time to linger. She gave one tear-blurred look about the old familiar homely room and passed out into the April sunshine. The barnyard was empty; the chickens were gone; even the dog was perched up in the wagon. All that was left was her flower garden, neglected of late. The very air was filled with suppressed emotion and sadness.

"The children were excitedly calling her. The men were ready; so she gave one last look at the old home, one last glance at her brave flower garden, and then resolutely climbed into the wagon and took her seat beside her husband . . . facing west".

Seven months later and almost two thousand miles away, Mary Denny would weep again when she first saw her new home... the roofless cabin in the cold November rain at a place the Puget Sound Indians called Smaquamox.

There were seven men, four women and four children in the little wagon train of four "prairie schooners". All of them might have been described by old John Denny, the wagonmaster, as "kissin' kin". They were all Dennys or Borens and, as one historian has written somewhat irreverently but with considerable accuracy, "Denny men sure went for Boren women".*

Arthur Denny, John's fourth son, had been the first to woo and win a Boren woman. In 1843, five years before his father married the widowed Sarah Boren, Arthur had married her eldest daughter Mary Ann. At the time the wagons set out from Cherry Grove they had two small girls, Louisa Catherine, seven, and Margaret Lenora, four. And Mary Denny was four months pregnant.

The youngest child to make the overland journey was six-week-old Loretta, the daughter of John and Sarah. After fathering eight sons, the patriarch of the family found himself the proud if somewhat awed father of a baby girl.

The third wagon carried Sarah's son, Carson Boren, a somewhat unlikely pioneer whom the children referred to as "Uncle Dobbins", his wife and small daughter, and Sarah's unmarried daughter Louisa, along with her mirror, Christmas presents and sweetbriar seeds, all of which were destined to become legendary in Northwest history.

The fourth wagon was occupied by John Denny's four younger unmarried sons, James, 27, Samuel, 24, David, 19, and Wiley, 17. The two eldest sons, Lewis and Alford, had not succumbed to the Oregon Fever, moving instead to Missouri. The third, John F., joined another overland train to Oregon a year later.

According to the methodical journal of Arthur Denny, which began: *"Journal of the Route to Oregon kept by A.A. Denny, April 10th, 1851, left home at 3 o'clock P.M."*, three of the wagons were drawn by four-horse teams and the other by a single span. There were also some saddle horses, several head of cattle and two watchdogs.

It has been generally assumed that Arthur Denny led the little band across the wilderness, probably because in his later years it was difficult to imagine that he had ever taken orders from anyone. Family records make it clear, however, that his father, the old Kentucky frontiersman and Indian fighter, was the "Captain".

Furthermore, although he didn't mention it in his later reminiscences, Arthur was laid low by that old complaint, the "ague", or by a new malady, "mountain fever" during much of that year.

Of the four unmarried sons, James, Samuel and Wiley were less than dedicated trailblazers. They performed their duties adequately, but by the time they had reached the relatively civilized valley of the Willamette in southern Oregon Territory they had had their fill of hardships and adventure and were not inclined to push further into the wilderness of the far Northwest.

Young David Denny, on the other hand, took to the Overland Trail like a duck takes to water. Possessed of seemingly unbounded physical vitality, he escaped the prevalent chills and fever until he reached the journey's end and cheerfully performed the duties of his ailing kinsmen as well as his own. A crack shot and an expert fisherman, he was the hunter who supplied the family with much of their food, the Indian scout, the handy man at camp sites and river crossings. And when the wagons were bedded down for the night he frequently stood double guard duty.

David's natural good nature was no doubt strengthened by the fact that the long journey west provided an excellent opportunity for him to continue the courtship of pretty Louisa Boren that had begun back in Cherry Grove, and under more romantic circumstances. The Illinois farm boy had become the rifleman of the Oregon Trail, the provider of food and the protector against wild beasts and hostile Indians.

The four wagons crossed the Mississippi River at Burlington and continued across sparsely settled Iowa. Three weeks after the departure from Cherry Grove they reached the last outpost of civilization, Kanesville, or Council Bluffs, just east of the Missouri River. After "resting up" for six days the wagons were driven aboard a steam ferryboat

---
*Sons of the Profits or, "There's No Business Like Grow Business! The Seattle Story, 1851-1901, by William C. Speidel, Nettle Creek Publishing Company, Seattle, Washington, 1967.

that carried them across the river to the eastern terminus of the old emigrant road that bordered the Platte River. The trail was easy to follow, for hundreds of other covered wagons had ground their way along it before them, leaving the double ruts of their iron-tired wheels, bordered by the narrower beaten path of the ox-drivers who had walked beside the plodding teams.

The Platte River was also a guide as well as a friend to the travelers. Called by the wagon train emigrants "the river that's a mile wide and a foot deep", it provided water that was muddy but drinkable, fuel from the willow and cottonwood groves along its banks, and sometimes a watery roadbed that provided cooling relief from the dusty trail. Once the wagons were in the water, however, it was important to keep them moving, for there were beds of quicksand at frequent intervals. The horses were always provided with their fill of water so they wouldn't be tempted to stop and drink along the way.

On one occasion, Carson Boren . . . Uncle Dobbins . . . who tended to be a little absent-minded at times, stopped his team in midstream for some unexplained reason and wagon and horses began to slowly sink beneath him. Fortunately the frantic shouts of the more alert pioneers roused him from his reverie in time to get moving again.

Over a period of many days Arthur Denny's concise journal recorded the party's close association with the river . . . *"camped on the river"* . . . *"drove on the river bottom"* . . . *"waded for willows for fuel"*. Finally, on Friday June 13, two months and three days from Cherry Grove, he wrote, *"camped on the river perhaps for the last time"*.

There would be weary days ahead when the parched and grimy pioneers would look back on that abundance of water, brown and muddy as it was, with nostalgic longing, but there were times along the Platte when they had received too much of a good thing.

During the early weeks of the migration, the women had insisted upon maintaining as far as possible the amenities of civilized life. Meals were served on neatly washed and ironed tablecloths and adults and children alike slept in modest white flannel nightgowns between linen sheets in neatly made beds, but such niceties ended on the far side of the Missouri River when a midnight thunderstorm blew down their tents and thoroughly saturated them and their belongings with a violent downpour of rain. It took several days to make repairs and dry out clothes, bedding and provisions. Thereafter, according to Louisa Boren's account as recorded in later years by her daughter Emily, they *"were glad to rest in the easiest way possible, when worn by travel and too utterly weary of the long day's heat and dust, with grinding and bumping of wheels, to think of the niceties of dainty living"*.

A few days later an equally sudden hail storm took the party by surprise and threw the horses into panic, prompting the usually laconic Arthur to record the event with unusual detail:

"Road & weather fine until about 3 o'clock when we had a hail storm which lasted but for a few minutes during which time there was the greatest confusion & everyone had enough to do to look to his own team & but little time to look at others; at one time I had almost given up my 2 horse team containing the family & nearly all the other valuables I possessed".

David took the near stampede in stride, although he had a four-horse team to keep under control. In later years he recalled modestly that *"the poor animals were quite restive, no doubt suffering much from their shelterless condition"*.

Generally, however, the Dennys and Borens found the countryside friendlier than their fellow emigrants in the Platte River country. Soon after crossing the Missouri they fell in with a much larger train of 18 wagons and it was decided to join forces for mutual protection.

John Denny was elected "Captain" or wagonmaster and took charge with the no-nonsense firmness to be expected of an old soldier and lifelong frontiersman. Although he leavened his discipline with the homespun Lincolnesque humor that had always warmed the hearts of those around him, discord soon arose. It became apparent that the occupants of the 18 newly joined wagons regarded themselves as rugged individualists who weren't inclinded to take orders from anybody. They argued with old John Denny over the evening stopping places, his choice of men to stand night guard and his insistence on getting under way early in the morning.

David T. Denny. *Louisa Boren Denny.*

He soon ran out of patience and informed the contentious ones in colorful language that he was "diselecting" himself from the position of wagonmaster. The strangers chose a successor from their own ranks, but he only succeeded in creating further dissension.

John Denny gathered the four original wagons and set out independently, vowing that he would never again join forces with such "'tarnal critters" as those, who could be heard shouting at one another in angry disputation long after their 18 wagons disappeared from sight behind the willow trees.

After camping for a day on "a willow island to bake bread and prepare for our journey over the plains", the wagons forded the Platte for the last time and entered the grim and barren wastelands of Wyoming Territory.

CHAPTER FOUR

From the Platte to the Columbia

Soon after leaving the willow groves of the Platte and entering the seemingly endless plains of Wyoming, the little band of pioneers from Cherry Grove were cheered by their first view of the Rocky Mountains, their summits shimmering like a mirage on the far western horizon. And for weary days and weeks thereafter that rugged continental divide held its mirage-like quality, seeming to retreat a mile for every mile the creaking wagons covered. It was almost a month after David Denny, scouting ahead of the train, galloped back excitedly to report the dream mountains on the horizon before the wagons attained the reality of their slopes.

Even then they seemed unreal to the Iowa prairie-dwellers, who had envisioned the Rockies as a single high ridge that could be easily climbed on one side and even more easily descended on the other, after which they would be in Oregon and could probably see the Pacific Ocean.

At first the plains provided more than adequate forage for the animals as well as the huge herds of bison that roamed them. One Sunday, with the train camped for the day to observe the Sabbath, a herd of bison was sighted for the first time. Hunger for fresh meat overcame the religious convictions of David Denny and Carson Boren, who were both enthusiastic hunters and fishermen. Mounting their horses, they headed for the herd, which was about three miles from the camp. Before they got there, hunters from another wagon train arrived and shot a couple of bulls, scattering the rest of the herd across the prairie. Although the earlier arrivals shared the meat with them, David and "Uncle Dobbins" were determined to make a kill of their own. Leaving their horses picketed on the plain, they began stalking a wily old bull that had become separated from the rest. They were unable to get closer than extreme rifle range. Shots were fired, but fortunately for the shaggy beast . . . and probably for his pursuers . . . they missed and he ran away unhurt.

After the heat of the chase had cooled, David conceded that "it might have been a very serious matter to have been charged by a wounded buffalo out on the treeless prairie where a man had nothing to dodge behind but his own shadow".

Gradually, as the seemingly endless pilgrimage toward the Rocky Mountains continued, day after weary day, the heat of the sun intensified, the grass and prairie flowers withered and died out and the prairie soil gave way to desert sand. It was here that the bitter hardships of the Oregon Trail were dramatized. On both sides of the trail were newly mounded graves and piles of household goods that earlier travelers had abandoned to lighten the loads of their exhausted horses and oxen. Even so, hundreds of the animals

Sarah Loretta Denny

collapsed and died, their whitening bones adding to the grim desolation of this cruel land.

The little band from Cherry Grove survived the perils of the trail without loss of life, but they did not escape illness. Arthur Denny continued to periodically suffer from the "ague", his wife Mary was not enjoying a comfortable pregnancy in the sweltering heat of a jolting covered wagon, and their two little girls, Lenora and Catherine, had suffered a long bout of whooping cough. According to family legend, the children had been told that they couldn't tell some of their Cherry Grove playmates goodbye because their friends had the whooping cough, but at the last minute, and before anyone could stop them, they jumped from the wagon and ran to kiss their little friends through the picket fence.

By the time the grassy prairie had begun to merge with the sandy desert, the two had recovered sufficiently to look forward to the evening halts as a time for play. They were delighted when they spied a big pile of white sand and were starting toward it when their mother called them back and warned them not to go away from the wagon. They found the temptation too great, however, and gradually edged their way toward the pretty sandpile while their mother was occupied with cooking the evening meal. No sooner had they reached it and begun to dig in it than they found themselves covered with huge biting ants. Their ensuing screams caused women to overturn cooking pots and men to grab for their rifles. Their Uncle David, who had been standing guard nearby, snatched them from the sand and carried them gingerly back to the camp, where supper was forgotten while everybody picked ants off the unfortunate children. According to Mrs. Watt:

"The friendly camphor bottle was brought out and both smarting bodies rubbed with camphor*, and the whimpering little girls put to bed. They learned their lesson well, for after that, no matter how tempting the sand pile or pretty the flowers, they never wandered from the wagons without permission".

On the far reaches of the western desert the wagon train took shelter from the burning sun as best it could during the day, getting under way late in the afternoon and traveling all night. One such nocturnal journey was described by David Denny's daughter Emily:

"Starting at four o'clock in the afternoon they traveled all the following night over an arid and desolate region, the Green River desert, thirty miles, a strange journey in the dimness of a summer night with only the starlamps overhead. In sight of the river, the animals made a rush for the water and ran in to drink, taking the wagons with them".

A major milestone along the way was Independence Rock, which towers seventy feet above the plain on the Sweetwater River near the present site of Casper, Wyoming. Independence Rock was known as the "Great Register of the Desert", for on its six-hundred-foot sides, the pioneers painted messages to record their passage. The children from Cherry Grove wanted to have their names added to the roster on the rock and it was, of course, Louisa Boren who helped them climb to a sufficient height and directed them in the proper spelling of their names.

From Independence Rock the party followed the Sweetwater to its source, high in the Rocky Mountains, discovering in the process that they were not coping with the kind of two-dimensional picturebook slope they had imagined, but a seemingly infinite range of peaks of a height and ruggedness never envisioned in their wildest dreams.

Finally, on June 21, 1851 . . . two months and eleven days after their departure from Cherry Grove, they reached the summit of the Rockies at South Pass. At that time Oregon Territory included the present states of Oregon, Washington and Idaho, as well as much of Montana, and the eastern boundary was on the continental divide. They had reached the Promised Land at last, but their journey was far from over. There were weeks more of dangerous, toilsome travel ahead before they could hope to reach the northwest outposts of civilization in the Willamette Valley.

The thickly wooded mountain country with its abundance of clear streams and rushing waterfalls, despite its hardships seemed a paradise after the grinding, sweltering weeks on the desert. The women were able to keep children, clothing and cooking utensils clean again and those indefatigable hunters, David Denny and Carson Boren were able to bring in game to add to the monotony of corn meal, flour, beans and bacon, which were staple food for the party. The nights were cold and patches of winter snow still lingered in places, but there was ample firewood and the children were happy to be relieved of their past chore of gathering dried buffalo chips to fuel cooking fires on the treeless plains. The days were warm and mountain flowers bloomed at the very edges of the snowfields.

Soda Springs on the Great Bear River was another long-remembered milestone along the weary way. The children were particularly fascinated by its wonders. They were amazed to find that the springs threw up boiling water in one place and icy cold in another, a fact that Lenora and Catherine again learned painfully. They decided to drink at a sparkling jet of water, only to find, too late, that it was almost boiling hot.

David Denny and Louisa went fishing on the Great Bear River and caught a fine string of beautiful speckled trout which, broiled over the embers of a pinewood fire, provided a rare treat for the whole party.

A few miles west of Soda Springs the trail forked, one branch dipping south toward California; the other northwest toward Oregon. Here the emigrants were met by guides from California, who expounded upon the vast riches to be had for the taking in the

---

*Camphor was a sovereign remedy of the Oregon Trail pioneers. An account of an earlier wagon train tells of a youth who was run over by a heavy wagon and suffered a compound fracture of the leg. When gangrene set in the leg was amputated with a butcher knife and meat saw. It was recorded that "laudanum was given, but without effect, the only other thing on hand to ease the pain was a bottle of camphor".

gold fields, but their sales pitch had no effect upon the Dennys and Borens. They had made up their minds long ago that Oregon, not California, was the Promised Land, and they held steadfastly to the Oregon Trail.*

A few miles northwest of the trail junction lay Fort Hall, a Hudson's Bay Company trading post on the upper Snake River in southeast Idaho. The Denny party arrived at that wilderness haven on July 4, 1851 . . . two weeks after reaching the summit of the Rocky Mountains and, according to Arthur Denny's calculations, 1,104 miles from Cherry Grove. Their arrival at the log stockade provided both encouragement and a heightened realization that they still had a long and hazardous way to go.

From here on they would follow the Snake River, which flowed northwest to the Columbia. They had accomplished two-thirds of their journey without fatal illness or a single hostile encounter with the Plains Indians.

At Fort Hall most of the wagon trains halted for a day or two to prepare for the final leg of their journey, and it was there that the more optimistic of the emigrants faced the fact that the most difficult and dangerous part of their long trek still lay ahead . . . nearly seven hundred miles of wilderness, blocked by scores of deep, swiftly-running streams, steep mountains and frequently hostile Indians. The stockade was surrounded by acres of abandoned wagons, household goods, tools and wagon parts. Faced with the stern realities of what lay ahead, the earlier wagon trains had discarded everything that wasn't considered absolutely essential to their survival.

But the Dennys and Borens didn't linger at Fort Hall. Their planning had been so thorough that it wasn't necessary to discard anything; not even Louisa's mirror. Their stock was in good condition and their sturdy wagons were not in need of parts from the vast junkyard outside the fort. They chose a camping place a mile or so beyond Fort Hall and young James Denny rode back to purchase a few supplies. The Hudson's Bay factor cautioned him that if they met Indians along the upper Snake "they must on no account stop at their call", for the Indians of that vicinity were "renegade Shoshones and horse thieves". He also provided John with a letter to be delivered to his father providing information on camping places where wood and water could be obtained between Fort Hall and The Dalles.

On the morning of July 5 an old Indian visited their camp and hung about all day. He seemed friendly and harmless enough, but David Denny kept a close watch over the camp that night. Apparently the old Shoshone had been detailed to check out the wagon train.

Things were peaceful enough that night, but the next morning as the women were preparing breakfast, a single young brave rode up with a string of ponies which, he explained, he wished to trade for Louisa Boren. He was deeply offended when his offer was firmly refused, becoming so angry and persistent that Louisa was afraid he would snatch her and gallop away into the wilderness. She hid herself in one of the covered wagons while David Denny stood guard and the rest of the party hastened to break camp and get the wagons under way "at a good smart pace". Even then the determined Indian refused to give up. He followed with his ponies for several miles before abandoning his courtship of Louisa.

After a long day of travel along the south bank of the Snake River, the party camped that night at the foot of American Falls. Again they enjoyed a peaceful night's sleep and arose at dawn to prepare for an early start. It was Sunday, a beautiful summer morning, and the scenery was lovely. There was an Indian encampment across the river, but there was no apparent activity there. In the deep pool below the falls they saw what appeared to be a flock of ducks bobbing along in single file.

As they contemplated the beauties of the scene the ducks became the black topknots of Indians, who rose from the water and rushed up the river bank toward the wagons, shouting that they wanted to trade. Their

---

*The south fork east of Soda Springs was also taken by some wagon trains headed for the Willamette Valley, following the "Applegate Trail", mapped by Jesse and Lindsay Applegate in 1846. Three years earlier they had lost a boat while shooting the rapids of the Columbia River above The Dalles while en route to the Willamette. Each lost a son and they determined to find a safer route. The Applegate Trail dipped south to cross northern Nevada, cut across the northeast corner of California and due north in Oregon from Lower Klamath Lake through Grants Pass to the Willamette. The earlier tragic loss of the Donner Party, which had taken an allegedly "shorter and safer" route to California, was well known to the pioneers of 1851 and doubtless influenced the decision of John Denny to stick to the traditional route to Oregon.

leader, who had apparently been lying in wait behind some rocks, popped up beside the lead wagon to the dismay of the modest ladies from Cherry Grove. His costume consisted of a stovepipe hat and swallowtail coat . . . and nothing else.

Old John Denny, the veteran cavalryman and Indian fighter, had grumbled over the instructions of the Hudson's Bay men to cut and run if they encountered Indians. He wasn't accustomed to running away from anything and it hadn't been easy for his sons to convince him that it was the proper strategy. The succeeding events proved how fortunate it was that they *had* convinced him.

As the drivers whipped up their horses, more Indians popped up from behind rocks and sagebrush and opened fire with rifles. Although Arthur Denny was suffering from the new miseries of "mountain fever", the episode was still vivid in his memory a generation later when he wrote his *Pioneer Days on Puget Sound*:

"On looking to the rear we could only see the puffs of smoke when they fired from behind the rocks, and at the same time we could hear the bullets whistle and see the dust fly where they struck, but fortunately they did not hit any of us".

The seven men of the party were armed with five rifles and two pistols, but only John, David and Arthur Denny and Carson Boren were marksmen, and Arthur was flat on his back with the ague. David, driving the lead wagon, and carrying a rifle and the two pistols, saw that more Indians were crossing the river, which was about two hundred yards wide, and running down the bank toward a ravine ahead. The trail led down one bank of the ravine and up the other and it was clear to David that their lives depended upon getting up the high bank before the Indians reached the ravine. He whipped up the horses to a gallop and the other drivers followed suit, the heavy wagons lurching and rocking and the terrified children clinging to their mothers. Sarah Denny was handling the reins of their wagon, leaving her husband John free to deal with the first hostile Indians who might get within range of his long rifle.

The careening wagons reached the bottom of the ravine ahead of the Indians and raced up the opposite slope to the top, where they found themselves with the tactical advantage of holding the upper ground from behind the shelter of numerous large rocks. To the delight of John Denny, they were in a position to stop and open fire, but the Indians were careful to keep out of range. After a period of armed stalemate the war party gave up and departed, leaving the little wagon train free to move on, which it did as rapidly as possible throughout the balance of that far from placid Sabbath day.

Not long afterward the Shoshones ambushed and massacred another small family wagon train in that same ravine.

After traveling until late that night to put as much distance as possible between themselves and the unfriendly Indians, the weary pioneers came upon a welcome sight . . . the cheerful light of a campfire reflected on the canvas tops of covered wagons. This was the small party of John N. Low . . . six men and two women from Ohio . . . who, it turned out, had crossed the Missouri just two days before the Denny party and traveled along the south side of the Platte while the Cherry Grove wagons held to the north side.

The women of the two parties evidently didn't meet until the next morning, for Mrs. Low said afterward that the first time she saw the women of the Denny party they were frying cakes over the campfire for breakfast. The emigrants from Ohio and those from Illinois hit it off well together and quickly agreed to travel henceforth as a single party. The decision may well have been strengthened by an incident recorded by Emily Denny in *Blazing the Way*:

"One of the women went down to the brook the next morning to get water for the camp and saw the tracks of Indian ponies in the dust on the opposite side of the stream. Evidently they had followed the train to that point, but feared to attack the united forces of the two camps".

Low, an easy-going man of 31, was an enthusiastic breeder of pure-bred cattle, and was driving the nucleus of his herd toward what he hoped would be the lush pastures of the Oregon country.

As the strengthened wagon train moved slowly across what is now southern Idaho and eastern Oregon, the pioneers learned that the Hudson's Bay factor at Fort Hall hadn't exaggerated the hazards and hardships of that region. They found that fording the swift mountain streams was far different from crossing the usually placid and shallow rivers of the plains. The wagon beds were made as watertight as possible with tar and tallow and floated across the deeper streams, while men and animals often had to swim. If the amphibious wagons weren't loaded heavily enough they tended to float off on the river current; if too heavily laden they might sink. There were close calls, but not a wagon or a head of stock was lost.

They also found the Blue Mountains considerably more difficult to cross than the Rockies. Men and beasts strained and sweated to inch the wagons up the steep slopes. Heavy chains wrapped around the trunks of trees were used as brakes to ease them down the breakneck grades. It took more than two weeks to reach the flatlands of eastern Oregon at Burnt River, where they were met by a party of some thirty Cayuse Indians; the advance nomadic tribe that was moving, "women, children, drags and dogs", from one summer camping place to another. The Cayuse braves were friendly, one of them announcing cheerfully, "Heap sleep now. We good Indians".

That was good news to David Denny, who, as one of the few not smitten by the mountain fever, had been standing double guard duty again all the way from American Falls . . . "one half of every other night and alternately slept on the ground under one of the wagons".

It was at Burnt River that a more significant meeting was held. Arthur Denny described it thus in later years:

"On leaving home for what we called the Pacific Coast, we had no other purpose than to settle in the Willamette Valley. But we met a man on Burnt River by the name of Brock who lived in Oregon City and had come out expecting to meet some friends, failing in which he turned and came back to the Dalles. He gave us information in regard to Puget Sound and called attention to the fact that it was about as near to the Sound from where we first struck the Columbia River, now known as Umatilla Landing, as it was to Portland, but as yet there was no road over the mountains by which it could be reached. My attention was thus turned to the Sound and I formed the purpose of looking in that direction".

When Arthur Denny "formed a purpose", he could be counted upon to follow it through. From the time of that chance meeting on the banks of the Burnt River with the "man by the name of Brock", the tiny wagon train from Cherry Grove was on a course that would lead it from obscurity to an enduring place in the history of the Pacific Northwest.

"Emigrant Train Attacked by Hostile Indians", from Ballou's Pictorial Drawing—Room Companion, *1857.*

CHAPTER FIVE

From the Columbia to Puget Sound

For days the wagons had rolled wearily through the hot, sandy desert of eastern Oregon, but on June 30 the party's advance scout, David Denny, galloped back with the welcome news that there was a change of scenery ahead. Gradually the sand dunes and sage brush gave way to struggling evergreens and before the day was over the train had progressed "over mountains and through a heavy pine forest which is delightful after traveling so long over barren deserts".

Six days later, on the first day of August, they "camped on the Umatilla bottom about five miles after striking it". It was here that the Oregon Trail reached the Columbia River gorge, but it would be another week before they reached trail's end at the river's edge.

The Umatilla Indians were both fishermen and farmers and they were eager to trade fresh food for clothing. John Low exchanged a well worn shirt for a huge salmon and Sarah Denny traded her second best apron for a mess of green peas. The fresh food tasted delicious, but after several days of repeated seafood dinners, Arthur and David decided to stalk the wily sage hens that abounded in the area and "have some chicken".

They brought back a fine brace of birds, but their hunting trip proved to be a waste of time. The sage hens had also gorged themselves on the overabundant salmon and tasted fishier than the fish.

After leaving the Umatilla, the wagons worked their way west along the river gorge, often in sight of the Columbia but high above it. The going was hard. At frequent intervals everybody had to get out and walk while the wagons were lifted and dragged over huge boulders in the trail. But at last, on August 11, 1851, they reached The Dalles, 1,765 miles and 80 days from Cherry Grove. The train had averaged 18 miles a day, which was considered excellent time by covered wagon standards.

The Dalles consisted of a scattering of traders' tents around an army outpost, but it was the nearest thing to an established community the travelers had seen since they crossed the Missouri River. They also found that "a man named Tudor" had several large open boats for charter. The mighty Columbia had, in the course of thousands of years, cut its own course through the last mountain barrier to the Pacific, the Cascades. Boats from The Dalles were able to reach the Cascades of the Columbia with relative ease, whereas wagon trains must climb the rugged Cascade Mountains over Barlow Pass.

It was decided to charter two of Mr. Tudor's boats to convey the women, children and much of the baggage downstream, while the wagons and all the men except Low, Carson Boren and Arthur Denny would proceed over the pass to Portland. Mary Denny was, by this time, in the late stages of pregnancy and was also deathly ill with mountain fever and it seemed doubtful that she could survive another mountain crossing.

It was David Denny's first parting from Louisa Boren since the long journey had begun, but he agreed that the plan was a good one. It would, he believed, spare her the hardships and dangers of the journey's final leg.

It didn't quite work out that way, however.

With their goal in sight, the pioneers wasted little time at the tent city of The Dalles. They spent the day of their arrival arranging for the boats and unpacking and separating the goods to be divided between boats and wagons. By nightfall the reorganization had been completed and the two boats pushed off. Arthur Denny, Boren and Low were in the smaller of the two, along with Mrs. Low, Mrs. Boren and three-year-old Gertrude Boren. The other women and children, including Sarah Denny and her baby daughter Lenora, and Louisa Boren occupied the larger craft. Both were filled with goods and supplies, leaving only enough room for the oarsmen. The passengers made themselves as comfortable as possible on top of the cargo.

The two crowded, topheavy craft soon became separated on the broad expanse of the river. The smaller one soon sprang a leak and Arthur Denny recorded in his journal, *"At about four miles we had to land and lie on the shore till morning in consequence of the boat leaking"*.

The passengers stumbled up the river bank in the dark, dragging or carrying the sleepy children, and bedded down as best they could for the night. There was no level ground and little Gertrude Boren rolled down the sloping bank and almost into the river before her mother caught her. In the morning, as they were breaking camp, they found a large rattlesnake neatly coiled alongside one of the beds.

The boat crew had repaired the leak, but soon after setting out they were forced to run into a creek for shelter from the rising wind. The weather improved at sunset and they reembarked, continuing down the gorge until midnight. The whistling winds of the mountain gorge continued to plague them and it was the morning of August 16 before they reached the Cascades.

The bigger boat had made the voyage in much faster time, but at considerably greater hazard to life and limb. In later years Louisa Boren told the story to her daughter, who recounted it in her book:

"She and the other women and children were in the larger of the boats. Wearied, most of them were asleep curled up as best they could on top of their plunder; but Louisa was wakeful and uneasy.

"From the time they started the boatmen had been passing a bottle among themselves which they called 'Blue Ruin'. A good name it was, for it nearly proved the ruin of all of them. 'Keep 'er goin', they kept singing foolishly.

"It was near midnight and the river was lighted by a waning moon. The solitary watcher noticed foam out in midstream and a distant hum caught her ears. The boatmen continued to pass the bottle and sing, 'Keep 'er goin'. The hum grew louder. Soon the waters had begun to roar, and Louisa realized all at once that they were nearing the rapids.

"She called to the crew to stop. They paid no heed. She frantically called her sister, 'Mary, Mary, wake up. We are nearing the falls. I hear them roar, and the men don't know what they are doing'.

"She climbed over the luggage, tugged at the boatmen, and begged them to pull for the shore.

"They answered, 'What's all the fuss about? There aint no danger, Miss. Keep 'er goin''.

"Her strong young arms grasped one of the men by the shoulder and shook him. 'Oh, man', she cried, 'don't you hear the falls? Look! Turn the boat to shore! Hurry or it will be too late'.

"Apparently not so drunk as the others, he awoke at last to the danger and said, 'My God, men, the gal is right. Make for the shore quick, none of us want to be drowned'. They pulled for the shore and landed safely some distance below the usual landing place. All were drenched. They built a fire, hung up their wet clothing and blankets on the bushes to dry, and camped there the rest of the night".

They had quite a story to tell when the rest of the party arrived at the Cascades four days later; one that could not but strengthen the conviction of the Denny men that alcohol was, indeed, the devil's brew.

"At the Cascades", Arthur Denny recorded, *"we found the first houses which looked really like civilization. F. A. Chenowith was*

building a tram road for the transfer of freight and passengers around the rapids, and at the upper landing were the Bradfords, Bush and Bishop, with others not now remembered. There was also a small side-wheel steamer, called the Flint, nearly completed, intended to run between the Cascades and the Dalles, in which service she entered that fall, but I do not now remember who built or owned her, but there can be no doubt of the fact that she was the first steam boat above the Cascades".

The reunited voyagers walked Judge Chenowith's tramway around the white water of the Cascades, their still damp possessions preceding them on a hand car. Below the rapids Chenowith's brig *Henry* lay moored, ready to carry them down the lower river and up the Willamette to Portland and, hopefully, a reunion with the overland segment of the party.

The *Henry* was a doubtful improvement over the bateaux that had carried them uncomfortably down river from The Dalles. An old New England cargo, drogher, she had made it around Cape Horn in 1846, but arrived on the Pacific Coast in such dilapidated condition that she was no longer fit for off-shore sailing, even by the sketchy safety standards of that era. After reposing on the mudflats of the Willamette for several years, she was acquired by Chenowith to transport supplies and building material for the construction of his tramway and to carry cargoes of salt salmon back to Portland.

After boarding this semi-derelict, the women made beds, as best they could, on top of the fish barrels in the hold, but worn out as they were they found it impossible to sleep because of the iron-staved barrels and the clouds of ravenous mosquitoes.

Viewing the ruins of the *Henry*, Arthur Denny was moved to one of his rare bursts of humor. He told John Low, who was the only one of the party who had been to sea, "Look here, Low, they say women are scarce in Oregon and we had better be careful of ours".

The bulwarks had long since rotted away from the *Henry's* decks and during the daytime the children had to be tethered to the masts with lengths of rope to keep them from falling overboard.

Helped along by both wind and current, the old brig reached Fort Vancouver on the lower Columbia the next day, but there she ran aground and lay all day on the mudflats until the tide came in again. Then the anchor was raised and she made it to the mouth of the Willamette, where she was anchored again for the night beneath a dreary downpour of rain.

The next day she got under way again, but again ran on the mudflats only three miles below Portland. The disgusted passengers left the listing hulk and found lodging for the night on shore. On Friday, August 22, according to Arthur Denny's journal, they "footed it up to Portland".

It was the 134th day of their journey from Illinois, one that could be made today by jet plane in a few hours.

At Portland, then an established city with a population of about two thousand, they were soon reunited with the overland members of the party, but they found the valley of the Willamette not to be the paradise they had expected. Most of the party suffered new and intensified bouts with the ague, shaking with chills one day and burning with fever the next. Fortunately for Arthur and Mary Denny, the malarial fever afflicted them on alternate days and they were able to take turns caring for each other. Arthur commented dryly that they were "always glad to share with each other . . . even the ague".

Even worse than the unhealthy climate of the river valley, as far as Arthur Denny was concerned, was the fact that the choicest claims had already been staked and the city of Portland platted by earlier arrivals. He hadn't traveled nearly two thousand miles at considerable risk to life, limb and health to buy city lots from somebody else. He recalled the glowing report of the man he had met on the Burnt River and concluded that it would probably make him both healthier and wealthier if he were to establish a city of his own in the Puget Sound country, where prime land was to be had for the taking and salt breezes were said to keep the air clean and salubrious.

---

*According to *Lewis & Drydens Marine History of the Pacific Northwest*, "The first steamboat on the middle river, the *James P. Flint*, appeared this year (1851). She was built at the Cascades by the Bradfords and Van Bergen, and after her completion was hauled up over the Cascades to run to The Dalles, where there was an established military post".

He and his wife were far too weak and ill to travel any further, but his younger brother David was more than ready to extend his scouting to Puget Sound. The sooner they settled down and got established, the sooner he and Louisa could get married. John Low was anxious to find winter pasturage for his cattle, so the two took a ferry across the Columbia and set out over the Cowlitz Trail toward Olympia, the principle settlement on Puget Sound.

Low found excellent range for his herd on Ford's Prairie on the Chehalis River and made arrangements to leave them there. Then he and David struck out again for Olympia, which was a village of a dozen cabins, a store or two, a post office and a customs house. They walked 200 miles over the winding trail, much of it through virgin forests so dense that the sunlight could barely penetrate at high noon.

Soon after arriving at the modest metropolis of Puget Sound, Low and Denny fell in with another man named Lee Terry who, with his older brother Charles, had left New York to join the California gold rush. Like most of the hopeful argonauts, they failed to strike it rich and had thereafter drifted apart, Charles stopping off at Portland and Lee pushing on to Puget Sound. Lee Terry had been reflecting upon the advantages of establishing a new town and when he learned that Low and Denny were going exploring for that purpose he cheerfully joined with them. The three made arrangements to voyage north with Captain Robert C. Fay, who was about to leave Olympia for the lower Sound to buy salmon from the Indians.

The leisurely voyage over the fifty-odd miles of inland sea between Olympia and Seattle was a pleasant one. Puget Sound is often at its best in the Indian Summer days of early fall, and David Denny decided that the man at Burnt River hadn't exaggerated the merits of this new Northwest frontier.

The broad-beamed clumsy boat moved slowly with the tide before a gentle breeze from the southwest. Blue-green forests were reflected in placid waters disturbed only by an occasional leaping salmon or inquisitive harbor seal bobbing up to inspect the passing boat. To the northwest lay the shining snow peaks of the Olympic Mountains and to the east the mighty cone of Mount Rainier.

The long northern twilight of the Puget Sound country was creeping in from the east when the boat slid in toward the forest-crowned beach near the site of what is now Fauntleroy in search of a camping place for the night. Darkness was already resting on the water, but the miles-high peak of Rainier was floating in a world of its own, the vanished sun still shining on its glaciers and fields of eternal snow.

As he rolled up in his blanket beside the driftwood fire below the primeval forest and the mighty mountain, and before he was lulled to sleep by the gentle surge of wavelets on the gravel beach, young David Denny told himself that he had, at last, reached the Promised Land.

Mt. Rainier from Lake Washington, Seattle.

Indian canoe on Puget Sound.

CHAPTER SIX

Birth of a City

It was a short and pleasant journey from the overnight campsite to their destination and on the early afternoon of September 25, 1851, Captain Fay swung the tiller and his clumsy craft lay over before the southwest breeze to round the headland the Indians called Smaquamox. Coasting along the gravel beach of the peninsula and along the southern shore of Elliott Bay, the boat rounded a bold headland and the muddy estuary of a sizeable river, the Duwamish, was revealed ahead. The gaff sail was furled, the oars manned, and the boat's blunt prow grated on the gravel beach just short of the river mouth.

David Denny, Lee Terry and John Low shouldered their packs and climbed ashore. Captain Fay and his crew shoved off and set out to secure their cargo of salmon for the San Francisco market, but the three pioneers were not alone on the shore of Elliott Bay. A party of Duwamish and Suquamish Indians were camped on the beach nearby, fishing for salmon. Their leader, a gray-haired patriarch of sixty who towered above his lesser tribesmen and wore his faded blue Hudson's Bay blanket like a Roman Emperor's toga, came down the beach to welcome the strangers.

The words of welcome were delivered in the language of the Duwamish, but there was no doubt that they were sincere. As David Denny clasped the hand of Chief Seattle he told himself that he would master the language of the Indian tribes. A better means of communication than sign language and the scanty Chinook trade jargon* would be needed if his people and those of Seattle were to live together in peace and harmony.

Reassured by the friendliness of Seattle and his people, the three explorers spent the night under a big cedar tree near where they had landed. The next morning they hired two young men of the Indian fishing party to take them up the Duwamish River in their dugout canoe, which was carved from a single cedar log.

The weather remained clear and bright, with a tang of fall in the air. To the easy dip of the paddles, the canoe glided up the river in the shadow of ancient firs and cedars. A few miles upstream they landed at the edge of a prairie where Low and Terry set out to explore an Indian trail that wound through the woods toward the back country. David Denny waited at the landing place with the Indians to make sure that they didn't decide to return home and leave the white men stranded.

Hours passed and the two explorers didn't return. The sun went down and the air grew chilly. What had begun as a delightful adventure was assuming the aspects of a bad dream. David shouted himself hoarse, then fired his rifle in the air, but there was no response. Finally he and the Indians returned down the river, dark and sinister now between its walls of towering trees. They made camp on another prairie, but there was no sleep for David that night. He had no way of knowing whether his friends were dead or alive, and he wasn't too certain of his own fate. His two Indian companions seemed friendly enough, but so had the Cayuse Indians at American

---

*This language of a few hundred basic words was developed by the early fur traders as a means of conversing with the Indians of the lower Columbia River and Nootka Sound. An earlier inter-tribal jargon was used, with the addition of some Latin, French and English words. Chief Seattle scorned this hybrid speech and, throughout his life, refused to speak in any tongue but that of his tribe.

Lee Terry.

Hudson's Bay Company steamer Beaver.

Falls . . . until they began shooting at the covered wagons.

At daybreak the next morning the Indians cheerfully launched the canoe and they headed back upstream in search of Low and Terry, whom they soon met coming down the river in another Indian dugout. They had had troubles of their own, it seemed. The Indian trail had petered out and they had blundered about in the woods until they came upon an Indian camp at the junction of Duwamish and Black Rivers, where they spent the night. The next morning their good-natured hosts provided a canoe and paddlers to take them back down the river for the reunion with the much relieved David Denny.

Early that evening they were back at their camping place on Elliott Bay. Captain Fay, who had been cruising about the adjacent waters buying salmon from the Indians, had returned and had a choice salmon roasting over the glowing coals of an alderwood fire. It was a far more cheerful evening than the previous one had been.

As they sat comfortably in the afterglow of sunset, sipping steaming black coffee and swapping tales of their recent adventures, they were amazed to hear the voices of men and women out on the bay. Sounds carry with remarkable clarity over the placid waters of Puget Sound, and it was apparent that the voices were those of white Americans. They hurried down to the water's edge and saw a scow being poled around Duwamish Head toward the river mouth. The voyagers saw the white men on the beach and worked the scow close inshore for a visit. The man with the pole introduced himself as Luther Collins and explained that he was returning from Olympia with his family and household goods after having staked a claim in the Duwamish River Valley. His wife and pretty fourteen-year-old daughter Lucinda had already learned the Chinook jargon and laughingly conversed with Captain Fay in the trade language.

Like most of the early pioneers of the Puget Sound country, Collins was an enthusiastic booster for the area he had chosen. He had first staked his claim on the Nisqually River near Olympia in the 1840's, but abandoned it to join the California gold rush. On his return he fell in with three other unsuccessful prospectors, Henry Van Asselt, Jacob Maple and his son Samuel, who planned to settle in the Willamette Valley. Frederick Grant, in his early *History of Seattle*, provided the following account of that meeting:

"*Collins, being a frank, open-hearted man, fond of talk, frequently told stories of the grand country on the Sound, the clams and oysters of the bay, the delightful climate, and the wild fruit and fowl and fish".*

Collins was as eloquent as Mr. Brock of Burnt River and the three men accompanied him to Puget Sound. When they couldn't find the land they wanted along the Nisqually, Collins told them of "a river valley forty miles down the Sound among the Duwamish Indians" and suggested they take a look at it. This they did and, according to Grant, *"on reaching the river they found it to be a full stream with extensive meadow lands or bottoms of the most fertile soil having certain grassy prairies".*

They staked their claims there . . . Maple on the prairie where David Denny had spent the lonely and wakeful night while his friends were lost . . . on September 14; eleven days before the arrival of Denny, Low and Terry on Elliott Bay. Van Asselt and the Maples had then returned to the Willamette Valley to move their families north, while Collins went back to the Nisqually Valley to sell his claim and likewise move his family to the Duwamish. It was on the return trip that he was hailed by David Denny and the others on the beach below Duwamish Head.

Collins pointed out that there was still plenty of good farm land available on the river and suggested that they join the settlement there, but David Denny and Lee Terry had determined that they were going to build a city and John Low had apparently caught some of their enthusiasm. A city should be on salt water with easy access to the sea, and on salt water they would stay.

It was getting dark by then. Collins gave up and the scow moved on down the shadowy shore, entered the river and disappeared from sight. It seemed a little less lonely under the cedar tree on the shores of Elliott Bay that night.

The next morning the little party moved back toward the harbor entrance and pitched camp near the tip of the curving peninsula the Indians called Smaquamox. Low and Terry were convinced that this was the ideal site for their future city. They were wrong, but their choice seemed logical enough. The land sloped gently to the deep waters of the Sound. It provided the only open space in the dense forest where they could build homes and lay out gardens, and it could be seen for miles by any ships that might pass. The two decided to stake their claims there and lay out a town site. Terry, in his unbounded enthusiasm, suggested that they name their city New York, for he was confident that it would some day rival that metropolis.

David Denny, who was still a minor, couldn't legally file a land claim for himself, but he didn't much care. All he really wanted was a plot of ground where he could build a home for himself and Louisa Boren, and Lee Terry's New York seemed as good a place as any.

Captain Fay had procured a full cargo of salmon and was anxious to get it back to Olympia before it spoiled. Low went with him to make the return journey over the Cowlitz Trail and get his family. Before he left he hired Denny and Terry to build a log cabin for him on his newly staked claim. As he walked the long trail alone he carried a letter from David Denny to his brother Arthur:

"We have examined the valley of the Duwamish River and find it a fine country. There is plenty of room for one thousand settlers. Come on at once".

Left alone on the beach, except for the constantly increasing assembly of Indians who seemed fascinated by their every move, David Denny and Lee Terry began building the new city's first permanent structure. Falling the trees and dressing the logs with only an axe, a hammer and their bare hands was hard work at best, and David soon discovered that he was bearing the brunt of it. Lee Terry was not an advocate of the American work ethic at any time, and he now viewed himself as a future merchant prince in a city he had founded and named. Sweating and straining over a pile of logs was bad enough, and he firmly refused to compromise his dignity further by involving himself in the preparation of meals.

Easy-going David Denny arose at dawn to build up the driftwood fire, fetch water and cook breakfast. After the day's work was over he was similarly occupied in cooking dinner, washing dishes and gathering wood for the next morning's fire while his companion eased his aching bones and grumbled at the harshness of frontier life.

After the first tiers of logs were laid they found it impossible to lift the others into place. They hired Indians to help, paying them in ship's bread, or hardtack.

While they were working on the cabin they again sighted their "neighbor", Collins, driving a herd of cattle along the beach aided by a Nisqually Indian known as Nisqually Jim. He explained that he had started out with them from Olympia in his scow, but that it had sprung a leak and sunk. The cattle swam ashore and completed their journey along the beach.

Soon afterward the two young men had less reassuring visitors. Awakened on a foggy morning by the thump of paddles and the chant of the Indian paddle song, they were startled to see a big war canoe loom out of the mist and grate ashore on the beach below their improvised lean-to of fir and cedar boughs. Led by a black-bearded chief, the strange Indians crowded around the shelter and tried to enter it, but Terry and Denny stoutly blocked the way.

The unwelcome visitors eventually left without calling the white men's bluff, but they were obviously a different breed from the amiable Duwamish and Suquamish. David later learned that these were Skagits from the northern Sound country and they seemed to bear out the truth of the adage that the further north one went, the more warlike the Indians became.

Despite such interruptions and a growing lack of enthusiasm for hard work on the part of Terry, Low's cabin was completed as far as the roof by late October, but that was as far as they could go. They didn't have a frow . . . the L-shaped tool used to split cedar shakes . . . and they couldn't complete the roof without one.

Mr. Collins had patched up his scow by that time and opportunely passed by on his way back to Nisqually. Terry hailed Collins down and drifted off in search of the needed tool. David was left by himself for the next three weeks.

With the coming of November the last traces of Indian Summer had vanished. A gray pall of clouds shrouded the shining mountains, chill winds swept the exposed peninsula, and steady, dreary rain beat down on the roofless cabin and the leaky lean-to.

A few days after Terry's abrupt departure the wet axe handle slipped in his hand and David slashed his foot so deeply that he was barely able to hobble about with the aid of an improvised crutch. Hungry, wet and cold, he finally fell victim to the malarial chills and fever that had for so long plagued the other members of the party and, for good measure, he was afflicted with a severe case of neuralgia.

He must have concluded that things couldn't possibly get worse when the family of skunks moved in and stole the last of his scanty food supply.

As Roberta Frye Watt wrote in later years, *"There he was under a shelter of cedar boughs with Indians camped about him and wild animals lurking in the woods. The ceaseless lapping of the water, the sighing and moaning of the wind, the hooting of owls, and the weird chanting of some brave on a distant shore only added to his loneliness. Surely this boy of nineteen needed all of his pioneer spirit".*

To young David Denny, in November, 1851, the Puget Sound country no longer seemed to be the Promised Land.

At about the time that Lee Terry embarked with Luther Collins in search of a frow, John Low completed his long hike from Olympia to Portland, delivered David's letter to Arthur Denny, and added his own enthusiastic praises of the townsite he and Terry had laid out on the shores of Puget Sound. Low had hitherto been interested only in finding good pasturage for his cattle, not a site for a city. Arthur concluded that they must indeed have come across a humdinger of a townsite and that they had better not waste any time in capitalizing on it.

The quickest means of getting there was Captain Isaiah Folger's little two-masted schooner *Exact*, which was moored on the Portland waterfront taking on passengers and freight for Puget Sound. Captain Folger had sailed the 73-foot craft from Nantucket around Cape Horn to California the previous year, reaching San Francisco at the height of the gold rush. The Yankee shipmaster had the good sense to stay away from the gold fields, entering the *Exact* in the highly profitable coastal trade. Now he was preparing to cash in on another gold rush, this one in the Queen Charlotte Islands of Canada. A party of hopeful prospectors had booked passage for themselves and their supplies, along with a number of emigrants bound for Olympia, but when Arthur Denny approached Captain Folger with cash in hand, the enterprising skipper decided he could find room for another ten adults, twelve children and their gear.

Although John and Sarah Denny and their two older sons had decided to stay in the Willamette Valley, the party that boarded

Drawing of schooner Exact *by Hewitt Jackson.*

the *Exact* on November 4, 1851, was half again as large as the one which had left Cherry Grove seven months earlier. For one thing, Arthur's wife Mary had given birth to a son soon after their arrival at Portland. Then there were John and Lydia Low and their four children, and another former Illinois farm family, William and Sarah Bell and their four children. William Bell was, at 34, the oldest member of the party. Like the Dennys and the Borens, the Bells had left their Illinois farm in the spring of 1851 as members of a wagon train bound for the Oregon country. A quiet, almost reticent man, Bell had listened to the increasingly enthusiastic talk of the Puget Sound country and quietly decided to throw in his lot with his friend, Arthur Denny.

Finally, by rather remarkable coincidence, there was Charles Terry, Lee's 22-year-old elder brother, who shared the family enthusiasm for storekeeping and had decided that the new town on Puget Sound might be a good place to set up shop. He had no idea that his brother was already there and had named the town New York.

And there was another coincidence. Captain Robert Fay had carried the party's advance guard to Elliott Bay and his future wife was also on board the *Exact*, although at the time she was Mrs. John Alexander and was on her way to the established town of Olympia with her husband and two young sons; she and Captain Fay hadn't even met.*

---

*The Alexanders stayed in Olympia until the spring of 1852, when they took up a 320-acre donation claim on Whidbey Island at the present site of Coupeville. John Alexander established a trading post there, dealing mostly with the Indians and the captains of incoming sailing vessels. In 1858 he suffered a fall on his dock that proved fatal. Mrs. Alexander married Captain Fay in September, 1860, and in later years became known to the pioneers of the Puget Sound country as Grandma Fay.

34

North Pacific Ocean off Cape Flattery.

Mrs. Alexander's 16-year-old son, John Sharp Alexander, had an observant eye, artistic talent and a love for ships. He made an accurate drawing of the *Exact* and gave it to his mother as a momento of the voyage and it remains the only authentic contemporary picture of the little vessel that had such an impact on the history of the Pacific Northwest.

His mother also had an eye for detail and a gift for recording the right things . . . how the women prepared for the sea voyage, what was served for breakfast on that historic morning of November 5, 1851, on board the *Exact*, the songs the prospectors sang . . . and another flash of grim humor on the part of the usually taciturn Arthur Denny.

It is fortunate that Grandma Fay left her warmly human account of that voyage, for none of the others ever displayed much interest in talking about it.

The *Exact* was due to sail on November 5 and the passengers brought their belongings aboard the day before. Grandma Fay recalled in later years that the women washed and starched their sunbonnets "very stiffly" and ironed them on the short grass of the river bank.

Charles Terry had invested his savings in the stock for the new business he planned for the new city and in the morning, shortly before sailing time, his goods were hoisted aboard, to be duly noted in his memorandum book:

1 box Tin ware
1 " Axes
1 " tobacco
1 Keg Brandy
1 " Whiskey
1 Box Raisins

Arthur Denny, the strict teetotaler, may have felt that the stock of their new city's first mercantile establishment was a bit heavy on alcoholic stimulants, but he was, above all, a practical man and he had learned enough about the Northwest frontier to be aware that high-proof liquid refreshments were considered by most of its inhabitants as essential to their survival and well-being. Not many of the thirsty pioneers would do their trading at a place where there wasn't a nip of something available to ward off the chill.

While Charles Terry saw to the safe stowage of his stock in trade and the Queen Charlotte-bound miners started a game of poker on deck, the women availed themselves of the opportunity to buy fresh provisions. Many years later Mrs. Alexander, as "Grandma Fay", recalled the subsequent events in detail and with a homespun sense of humor:

"The morning we came on board the schooner to come to the Sound some Indians came along with some salmon, and we all bought some. The stove was small and so I let the others cook their breakfast first. We couldn't all cook at once and so I fixed up my two little boys and attended to some other work. Well, the rest all got through and I was just going to cook my salmon when I began to feel sick. I didn't any more than have to look around before I see that I wasn't alone. Everybody was sick together.

"The Dennys had their bunk on one side of the stove and I had mine on the other. I guess I never will forget Mr. Denny lying there, and every time he'd get so he could speak he'd look across at me with a kind of twinkle in his eye and say: 'What are you lying there for, Mrs. Alexander? Why don't you get up and cook your fish?'

"Them that stayed on top didn't get sick, and Mr. Terry was among them. I don't know whether he thought he'd celebrate having got over the plains safe or not, but anyway he told the men that he had some good cigars in his chest and he'd go down and get them. So down Mr. Terry comes, and he hadn't any more than stooped over and unlocked his chest than he got sick, and instead of taking his cigars up to the boys he crawled into his bunk, about as sick as any of us. The men on top, not being sick, could afford to have a little fun, so they all kept looking down at Terry and calling out: 'Hurry up with them cigars you went after, Terry. What are you doing down there Terry?'"

Among those who wisely stayed "on top" as the *Exact* left the placid waters of the Willamette and began lifting to the ocean swells of the lower Columbia were the jolly miners, who continued to entertain themselves with cards and song. Their favorite ditty was "Three Blind Mice", which they sang over and over "until their voices seemed to rise and fall with the swell of the sea".

In later years the occupants of the crowded, salmon-scented quarters below recalled the miners' musical efforts as "almost as much an affliction as seasickness".

On November 7, the *Exact* was cleared by the customs officials at Astoria, just inside the Columbia River bar, and proceeded to plunge and buck her way across the huge swells and swirling currents at the river mouth. She made it safely and for the next four days on the open Pacific the passengers remained only normally seasick. On November 11 the little schooner rounded Cape Flattery and entered the protected waters of the broad Strait of Juan de Fuca. The pilgrims below decks began to believe that they might live after all.

The *Exact* scudded smartly up the Strait as far as Dungeness, where the wind deserted her and she lay becalmed for 24 hours. Captain Folger had two other old master mariners on board as passengers and self-appointed consultants, but none of the three had ever sailed the inland waters of Puget Sound. Captain Fay, in the course of his small boat voyages of exploration and salmon-buying, came across the schooner at anchor and Captain Folger asked him to pilot the vessel through the Sound to Olympia.

It was while performing this service that Captain Fay met Mrs. Alexander and, according to family legend, said, "To think that when I meet the most charming woman the whole world over it is on board the *Exact* and she is the wife of another man".

David Denny, keeping his lonely and uncomfortable vigil at Smaquamox was also convinced that Captain Folger's schooner carried the most charming of women, and so the *Exact*, carrying Frances Alexander and Louisa Boren to meet their future husbands, brought the makings of storybook romance as well as the makings of a great new city.

At three o'clock on the wet dark morning of November 13, a northwesterly breeze sprang up and all hands were called to make sail. By the time the anchor was catted and the sails trimmed, the breeze had become a half gale and the *Exact* was running before the wind with a fine bone in her teeth. Dawn found her storming up Admiralty Inlet at a good 10 knots.

John Low, as the only other man aboard who had ever seen Smaquamox, or "New York", as Lee Terry had by then christened it, was on deck with Captain Fay keeping an anxious lookout for the infant townsite. The forest-crowned bluffs, veiled by rain and low-scudding clouds, looked disturbingly alike.

Then the *Exact* foamed past a high point of land and swung into a broad bay. The steep bluffs ended in the wet mudflats of a river estuary, another bold headland and a gently sloping shore that thinned to a gravel beach. The blurred landscape came into focus and was suddenly identifiable as Elliott Bay, the twin mouths of the Duwamish River and the peninsula the Indians called Smaquamox.

Finally, as the schooner approached the far shore, Low saw the wet shine of peeled logs between the forest and the beach, but upon closer inspection he felt his heart sink. The cabin was roofless in the driving rain and there were no signs of life about it. It appeared that David Denny and Lee Terry had given up and abandoned the place . . . or had been killed by Indians.

While John Low wiped the rain from his eyes and tried to solve the mystery, Captain Folger shouted his commands. The helmsman swung the tiller over and the schooner rounded up into the wind, well out in the Sound off the point. The last of her sail, the big single jib, came down and the anchor was let go with a metallic roar of chain.

It was eight o'clock on the morning of November 13, 1851, and the long journey from Cherry Grove, Illinois had ended.

* * * * * * * * * * * * * * * *

William N. Bell.

> "We have examined the valley of the Duwamish river and find it a fine country. There is plenty of room for one thousand settlers.
> Come at once."

Facsimile of Original note sent by David Denny to his brother Arthur

The harsh echo of the cable chain awakened David Denny from his fitful and feverish sleep. He wrapped himself in his wet blanket, fumbled about for his tree limb crutch and stumbled toward the beach, his aching jaws tied up in an old bandana handkerchief. The night before he had brewed the last of his tea, drank it scalding hot and crawled under his sodden blankets to sink into a long sleep of weakness and exhaustion.

The ubiquitous Mrs. Alexander was on deck to watch the landing of the pilgrims. She was bound for the relatively civilized town of Olympia and she felt sorry for the women who were landing in that howling wilderness:

"The wind blew and when the women got into the little rowboat to go ashore at Alki, they broke down and cried, every one of them, and the rain pelted down and their sunbonnets went flip flap, flip flap, as they rowed for the shore".

The sight of the roofless cabin, the scarecrow figure of David Denny and the aftermath of six solid days of seasickness were not calculated to make the occasion a cheerful one at best. The unending rain and the arrival of Chief Seattle's Indians, most of them naked and well annointed with layers of rancid dogfish oil, added nothing to it.

It was too much for even David Denny, who had viewed the hardships of the Oregon Trail as a continuing lark and who should have been cheered by the arrival of Louisa Boren and an ample supply of food.

"I wish you hadn't come", he told his brother Arthur as they met at the water's edge.

"But I'm glad to see you", he added after a moment's reflection. "The skunks have gotten in and eaten all my provisions".

And that was the nearest anybody came to making a speech at the birth of the city that would become Seattle.

Detail from Alki Point Landing Diorama, Museum of History & Industry.

Denny Cabin.

Monument marking Alki Point landing of the Denny Party.

CHAPTER SEVEN

New York Alki

By the time the *Exact* dropped anchor in Elliott Bay to unload the pilgrim party and their belongings Mrs. Alexander had recovered pretty well from her seasickness and the effects of Arthur Denny's humor during the salmon cooking fiasco in the schooner's cabin. She was going on to the civilized village of Olympia and she watched the drama of Seattle's founding with compassion as well as her usual eye for detail . . . the women weeping in the crowded longboat and their tears being washed away by the unending rain; Mrs. Denny and Mrs. Boren and Mrs. Bell each carrying a baby in her arms and Mrs. Low trying to comfort a two-year-old girl. Their possessions had been piled at the water's edge and the tide was coming in. The men were trying to rescue the boxes and chests before they were carried away by the tide or the curious Indians who didn't know they were watching a great city being born.

If Mrs. Alexander said that all the women of the landing party were weeping as they left the *Exact* she was probably right, for she was a born reporter, but Louisa Boren may have been using her handkerchief to wipe away rain and not tears. At any rate, she was cheerful enough once she reached shore. Young David Denny, shivering in his soggy blanket and hobbling down the beach to meet her on his improvised crutch, wasn't exactly an inspiring sight to most of the party, but Louisa loved him and he looked wonderful to her. The girl who had carried a pocketful of sweetbriar seeds over the Oregon Trail was fascinated by the green vegetation of the strange new land . . . graceful sword ferns, salal, wild huckleberry and tiny mushrooms forming fairy circles in the delicate green moss. She examined each plant with the enthusiasm of a dedicated botanist. Toward evening the setting sun broke briefly through the dark clouds to the west and its rays momentarily illuminated the weathered cedar of an abandoned Indian camp across the bay. It was the only structure in the otherwise unbroken forest that towered above the eastern shore of Elliott Bay, and Louisa Denny was convinced that the brief ray of sunlight upon it was a good omen for the future.

The men of the party had little time to inspect the vegetation or admire the momentary sunset. They had their hands full rescuing their collective belongings and improvising some sort of shelter from the elements and the growing throng of odoriterous Indians. David Denny had cut up a cedar tree into bolts before he injured himself and a frow was included in Arthur Denny's tool box. (Lee Terry was still presumably wandering about on the upper Sound in search of this essential implement). By nightfall half the cabin roof was completed and the 24 men, women and children huddled together in the only reasonably dry spot in 500 square miles of rain-soaked forest, beach and mudflats.

The next day the cabin roof was completed and Mary Denny's cook stove (the only one in town) was set up in the middle of the one room. As the wet walls and floors dried and the cabin was filled with the pleasant odors of communal cooking, things looked considerably better to the citizens of New York West . . . especially to David Denny, who hadn't had a decent meal in days.

But even by frontier standards, those first weeks were hard. As Roberta Frye Watt wrote:

"Neither men nor women of this group of pioneers were robust when they landed. Although they were young . . . Mr. Low and Mr. Bell being the only two over thirty . . .

they were worn by the trip across the plains, and weakened by the ague and the recent trying experience of seasickness. Mary Denny and Sarah Bell were especially frail."

Furthermore, the growing band of Indians that surrounded them constituted an unknown factor. Although they seemed to be more a nuisance than a menace, they outnumbered the settlers by at least 200 to one and it was obvious that if they chose to turn against the trespassers on their ancestral lands, the new town . . . and its inhabitants . . . would be short-lived. Even Arthur Denny, who rarely admitted to any misgivings, conceded that he had had his doubts about the situation at Smaquamox in November, 1851. In an interview four decades later with Seattle historian Frederick Grant, he said:

"We were landed in the ship's boat when the tide was well out, and while the men of the party were all actively engaged in removing our goods to a point above high tide, the women and children had crawled into the brush, made a fire and spread a cloth to shelter them from the rain. When the goods were secured I went to look after the women, and found on my approach, that their faces were concealed. On a closer inspection I found that they were in tears, having already discovered the gravity of the situation. But I did not, for some time, discover that I had gone a step too far; in fact it was not until I became aware that my wife and helpless children were exposed to the murderous attacks of hostile savages that it dawned upon me that I had made a desperate venture. My motto in life was never to go backward and in fact if I had wished to retrace my steps it was about as impossible as if I had taken up my bridge behind me. I had brought my family from a good home, surrounded by comforts and luxuries and landed them in a wilderness, and I did not think it at all strange that a woman who had, without complaint, endured all the dangers and hardships of a trip across the great plains, should be found shedding tears when contemplating the hard prospects then so plainly in view."

Only David Denny and Louisa Boren seemed unimpressed by the hardships and potential dangers of those earliest days on Puget Sound. They were in love with each other and they soon began a love affair with the green and beautiful land around them which would

Henry Yesler.

last all their lives. Even fifty years later David's recollections revealed no hint of the momentary despondency which had prompted him to tell his brother, "I wish you hadn't come."

On September 25, 1901, a Seattle *Daily Times* reporter interviewed David Denny on the fiftieth anniversary of his landing, with Low and Lee Terry, at Smaquamox. His reminiscences were matter-of-fact and without reference to such minor irritations as sickness, injury, hunger or fear of the unknown. He recalled that *"looking out over Elliott Bay at that time the site where Seattle now stands, was an unbroken forest with no mark made by the hand of man except a little log fort made by the Indians"* . . . the place where Louisa Boren had seen the lucky ray of sunlight.

Of the building of the first settlement on what is now known as Alki Point* he said only:

---

*Alki, a word of the Chinook jargon meaning "bye-and-bye," was pronounced Al-kee by Indians and pioneers, but has over the intervening years been corrupted by common usage to Al-ki.

*"We built up quite a settlement over on Alki, and the Indians of course came and settled around us. No, we were not molested to any great extent. I remember that on one night, our women folks missed a lot of clothing they had hung out to dry, and I at once went to their big chief (Seattle) and told him what had happened. In a very short time not only were the missing articles returned to us, but a lot that we didn't know were gone. *"*

By the end of the second day the cabin of John Low had not only received a tight roof of cedar shakes, but several dozen Douglas firs had been felled, trimmed and peeled to build a second cabin for Arthur Denny and his family.

Although the white settlers worked from dawn to dark, the Indian community around them grew much more rapidly than their own. The Suquamish and Duwamish were attracted to Smaquamox both by a childlike curiosity and the belief that the white men's guns would furnish protection from the more warlike tribes from the north who frequently raided Puget Sound in their seagoing war canoes in search of slaves and booty. The Indians came by the hundreds, bringing their portable houses of split cedar and mats with them and setting them up on the land the white men had cleared.

The squat canoe Indians were both helpful and, as David Denny had indicated, annoying to the city-builders. They helped the settlers lift logs into place, bartered fresh salmon and venison for old clothes and ship's bread, taught the former inland farm people to dig and prepare clams and provided them with transportation in their dugout canoes.

They also distressed the straight-laced Victorians with their nakedness, their pervading odor of smoked salmon and rancid dogfish oil and their almost superhuman curiosity. They were even more interested in details than was Mrs. Alexander . . . what the white people ate and how they cooked it, where they slept and how their household utensils worked. Not infrequently, when the 24 white inhabitants were crowded into Low's one-room cabin for the evening, they would be joined by visiting Indians, fragrant with dogfish oil and sprightly with fleas; as many as fifty jamming themselves inside "until there would not even be room to scratch."

It probably occurred to neither whites, nor Indians that each was intruding on the property of the other.

Among the many things the settlers learned from the Indians was the easy splitting of long, wide boards from the straight-grained cedar trees, many of which were 200 feet tall and ten feet or more at the base. When Arthur Denny's cabin was finished and there were no more suitable logs in easy reach of men working without horses or oxen, they adopted the building techniques of the aborigines, Arthur Denny recalling that, *"we split cedar and built houses for Bell and Boren which we considered quite fancy, but not so substantial as the log houses."*

By the beginning of December the grandly titled settlement of New York, previously called Smaquamox, could boast four hourse and the beginnings of a general store being erected by Charles Terry with the reluctant assistance of his younger brother Lee, who had wandered back without a frau.

So far the budding townsite had attracted little attention from passers-by on the Sound. Only a few days after the landing from the *Exact* two men, F.W. Pettygrove and L.B. Hastings, landed on the beach from an Indian canoe. Room was made for them at the community dinner table and they spent the night rolled up in their blankets on the floor. The next morning they set off again to stake claims at another new town 40 miles down the Sound at Port Townsend, founded earlier in

---

The clothing of the white settlers was much coveted by the Indians and cast-off garments were a frequent item of barter with them. Chief Seattle, a strong believer in law and order, frowned on theft, especially from the whites. Mrs. Alexander described old Seattle's reaction to a similar theft from a clothesline in her usual colorful style:

"I never can forget how old Chief Seattle scared me once. He and his tribe were camped that winter where Olympia is now and our little log house stood right on the edge of their camp. They were quiet and peaceful and I wasn't afraid. One day I bought a new clothesline and put it up and hung out some wash. The next morning it was gone. We were sure the Indians had taken it and I went to see Seattle about it. He was sitting mending his pants. He just grunted. Then he drew in a big, long breath and gave a scream like I'd never heard. I was scared almost to death and nearly fainted. Every Indian in the tribe came running to where we stood. There they came, old and young. Old men crawled and young men ran like horses. Old women and young women, carrying babies and little children, came, along with dogs and everything that was alive in the camp.

"I didn't know whether I'd made him mad and they were going to kill me then and there. But that wasn't it. Old Seattle barked something at them that I couldn't understand, and every one of them disappeared as quickly as they had come. As soon as the way was clear I got to my house in a hurry, but I'd no sooner stepped in than an Indian came and handed me my clothesline. And that was the last thing I ever had stolen."

the year by Alfred Plummer and Charles Bachelder.

At rare intervals the settlers sighted sailing ships passing out on the Sound beyond the bay, and once or twice the Hudson's Bay Company's primitive side-wheel steamer *Beaver* trailing wood smoke from her tall funnel as she trundled on her way between Fort Nisqually and Victoria, but none came within hailing distance until December 10. On that day a brig, making a broad reach across the Sound, sailed close enough to the point that her crew could see the four cabins, the partly completed store and white men on the beach. The mainsail was backed, a boat was lowered and Captain Daniel Howard of the brig *Leonesa* was rowed ashore. He introduced himself to the settlers and asked them the name of their town.

They told him it was New York, and Captain Howard was polite enough not to laugh. Instead, he told them that the former shanty town of San Francisco was fast developing from a gold rush camp to a permanent city. New wharves were being built all along the waterfront and he had brought the *Leonesa* to Puget Sound in search of a cargo of piles. But the Sound was a mighty big place and he didn't quite know where to begin looking. And, he added, he had cash money in the ship's safe to pay for the cargo once it was delivered.

The young men on the beach didn't take time to discuss the matter. They just looked at each other and nodded and their senior citizen, John Low, spoke for them. He congratulated Captain Howard on having found exactly the right place along Puget Sound's two thousand miles of shoreline, and assured him that the men of New York were ready and willing to get out a cargo of good Douglas fir piling for the *Leonesa*. They signed a contract on the spot and the men . . . all except Lee Terry . . . got out their axes and sharpened them to a fine edge, congratulating each other on the fact that, less than a month after its founding, their town had its first maritime commerce.

There were enough trees close to the water's edge to supply the 50-foot piles specified by Captain Howard and they now had the assistance of a single yoke of oxen that Low had brought up from their winter pasture on the Chehalis River. This was adequate for

Loading timber on brig Leonesa.

their own land clearing and cabin building, but not for commercial logging operations.

Lee Terry predictably volunteered to go to the Puyallup Valley to buy another yoke of oxen, while the rest of the men set to work with what they had. He returned a few days before Christmas, driving the oxen along the beach, and while he rested from his journey, the others completed the loading of the *Leonesa* on New Year's Day, 1852. Captain Howard was pleased with the dispatch with which the amateur loggers had provided his cargo and promised to put in for another load on his return voyage. Before he left he duly paid for the piling in hard cash . . . a thousand dollars for the cargo which was sold a week or two later in San Francisco for $6,800. The basis of successful trade had been established. Both parties were satisfied with the deal.

Arthur Denny was even more pleased than the others. Captain Howard had expected to have to cruise around Puget Sound to acquire a full cargo and, like most of the shipmasters of that day, he had brought along a large stock of goods to sell along the way. With the limited market at New York he was left with a large surplus, which Arthur offered to take off his hands. There was plenty of room in his cabin now that the other dwellings had been completed and he was willing to take the goods on consignment, sell them for a percentage of the gross, and settle accounts when the *Leonesa* returned.

That provided New York with two stores, but Arthur had the advantage. Charles Terry had paid cash for his merchandise. The astute Arthur got his without making any monetary investment.

This probably widened the rift between the Terry brothers and Low and the rest of the founders of New York. The town boundaries had been staked by Terry and Low and when Indian treaties and formal land laws took effect it would be their town. Arthur Denny, unlike his easy-going younger brother, wasn't satisfied to settle for a couple of lots in somebody else's town. Furthermore, he and David had already decided it wasn't the proper place for a seaport. They were inland farmers who had never seen salt water until the *Exact* crossed the Columbia River bar, but they weren't lacking in common sense. The exposed point and shallow water just didn't seem right to them. After the arrival of the *Leonesa* they spent whatever spare time they had paddling about the Sound in an Indian canoe looking for a better location for a seaport city.

Under those circumstances it is likely that the Seattle *Post-Intelligencer* was guilty of romanticizing things a bit when, a half century later, it published a nostalgic feature story on those early days, concluding that the Dennys, Borens, Bells, Lows and Terrys "*made a happy little family.*"

Whatever their personal disagreements may have been, however, all the two dozen men, women and children of the settlement gathered together amicably for their first Christmas in the Promised Land, and it was a memorable one, although the men could take

Lee Terry

only a half day off from their timber cutting. (Charles Terry's notebook shows that on Christmas Day they "worked half a day and cut 11 sticks, 561 feet").

David Denny, the town's best marksman, had gotten up early to bag a brace of prime fat wild geese and Louisa Boren had, of course, been even more foresighted, bringing her small gifts across the plains and mountains months before in anticipation of the day.

Of that happy occasion, the late Seattle historian Nard Jones wrote in the *Post-Intelligencer* 108 years afterward:

"*Somewhere in the world, every year, there is a 'first' Christmas, in celebration of that first Christmas of all, in Bethlehem. So it has been since the birth of Jesus, and so it was on December 25, 1851, at Alki Point where Seattle began.*

Henry Van Asselt.

" 'On Christmas Day,' Mary Denny would one day tell her granddaughter proudly, 'everyone appeared bright and gay in clothes that were clean and whole.' By which she meant that there had been washing and patching and mending, but nothing new to wear.

"And they celebrated Christmas dinner together with wild goose as the main dish, pieced out with salmon. There were still a few dried apples in the bottom of a barrel brought from the *Exact*. As usual, clam broth served as milk for the infants. One record says that two bachelors, Sam Maple and Henry Van Asselt, were 'company' from the Duwamish settlement. But if they sought to get ahead of David Denny for the hand of Louisa Boren they were too optimistic.

"Of course it was the one who glimpsed the shaft of sunlight in the dark day of their arrival who also remembered there would be a first Christmas in a new and lonely land. Louisa had tucked away with the wall mirror, and her sweetbriar seeds, some small trinkets for the children, keeping them hidden until this Day of days."

It seems likely that the two lonely bachelors from the upper Duwamish were interested in more than a roast goose dinner, for as Emily Inez Denny wrote of her mother, Louisa:

"As she was strikingly beautiful, young and unmarried, both white and Indian braves thought it would be a fine thing to win her hand", but she added, *"the white competitors found themselves distanced by the younger Denny, who was the first of the name to set foot on Puget Sound."*

A number of the young braves of Seattle's confederated tribes also actively courted Louisa in their own way. The settlers were puzzled at first when the Indians kept bringing long poles and leaning them up against Arthur Denny's cabin where Louisa was living. When it was learned that these were courtship poles and that Louisa was expected to select one to signify her choice of its owner as her husband, David was faced with another after-hours chore; removing these symbols of savage admiration from the doorstep of his beloved and chopping them up for firewood.

After a while the Indian suitors either got the message or ran out of courtship poles and gave up, but David was convinced that the sooner he could get some land and build a honeymoon cottage the better. As his brother had commented with wry humor on the rainy morning of the landing from the *Exact*, "They say white women are scarce out here. The best thing we can do is to go to work to provide shelter for those we have."

While the ebullient Charles Terry occupied himself with the promotion of his town, the Denny brothers, Boren and Bell explored the Sound as far south as Commencement Bay and east to Port Orchard. They paddled up the Duwamish and its tributaries and explored the present site of Puyallup, but they didn't find what they were looking for. Finally, as a last resort, they went exploring closer to home, paddling around Duwamish Head and skirting the vast mudflats of the Duwamish River delta to a small headland near the center of Elliott Bay's eastern shore. The place was marked Piner's Point on the beautifully detailed chart prepared by Lieutenant

Wilkes' navy cartographers ten years earlier, but none of the explorers knew that such a chart existed. If they had, they would have saved themselves a lot of paddling.

Just off the point they discovered a small island of about eight acres where they had assumed there was nothing but mudflats. Between the island and the point was a salt water tidal lagoon. From that perspective they could see that they had been right about Terry's exposed point that jutted out into the Sound. It wasn't really a harbor at all, but the southern breakwater of the true harbor, taking the pounding of the winter storms and protecting the six-mile-wide entrance to the bay. Furthermore, this section of the bay was walled on three sides by seemingly unlimited timber ready to be felled directly into salt water. The only question was whether the water was deep enough to float seagoing ships.

The explorers had taken along a hundred-foot length of Mary Denny's clothesline and some horseshoes as an improvised sounding lead and when they put it to use they were surprised to find that the horseshoes took the line all the way down to the bitter end without touching bottom. Even close off the island the strong seaward set of the Duwamish River current had dredged a natural channel providing nearly forty feet of water.

After two weeks of earnest discussion, Arthur Denny, Boren and Bell went back across the bay and staked their claims on 320 acres each (160 acres for themselves and 160 for their wives) along the waterfront for a couple of miles on each side of "Denny's Island".

It was really on that day . . . Sunday, February 15, 1852 . . . that the town of Seattle was born, and for the next five years or so it would be engaged in all-out battle with Terry's New York for survival.

For a while it looked as if Terry's town would win out. When the *Leonesa* returned in April, she carried a greatly expanded stock of goods for the store that he and Low were operating. When the first issue of the Puget Sound country's first newspaper, the *Columbian*, datelined "Olympia, Puget's Sound, Saturday, September 11, 1852", appeared, it carried a sizeable advertisement for the "New York Makkook House".* The text, no doubt penned by Terry himself, was as follows:

NEW YORK MAKKOOK HOUSE.

CHAS. C. TERRY & CO., thankful for past favors take this opportunity to inform their numerous friends and customers that they still continue at their well known stand in the town of New York, on Puget's Sound, where they keep constantly on hand and for sale, at the lowest prices, all kinds of merchandize usually required in a new country.

N. B. Vessels furnished with cargoes of Piles, Square Timber, Shingles, &c.

New York, Sept. 1, 1852.   1tf

Advertisement for Terry's store in first issue of the Columbian.

"Chas C. Terry & Co., thankful for the past favors take this opportunity to inform their numerous friends and customers that they still continue at their well known stand in the town of New York, on Puget's Sound, where they keep constantly on hand and for sale at the lowest prices, all kinds of merchandize usually required in a new country.

"N.B. Vessels furnished with cargoes of Piles, Square Timber, Shingles & c. New York, Sept. 1, 1852"

Although the "New York Makkook House" prospered, particularly in its dealings with the simple Indians, Charles Terry soon became aware that his choice of a name for his town wasn't selling at all on the rugged Northwest frontier. Most of the pioneers didn't like big cities, which was the reason they had come to the Puget Sound country in the first place, and they didn't take kindly to the Terry brothers' grandiose title for their wilderness trading post. Most of them made fun of it by tacking on the Indian word meaning bye-and-bye, making it New York Alki. The Chinook jargon, with its limited vocabulary, made use of tone and inflection to make its finer points. The slower the world "alki" was drawn out the further the bye-and-bye became. The settlers from other aspiring settlements *really* drawled it out, a form of humor which annoyed the Terrys exceedingly.

Makkook or *Mahkook*, Chinook jargon world meaning to buy or sell.

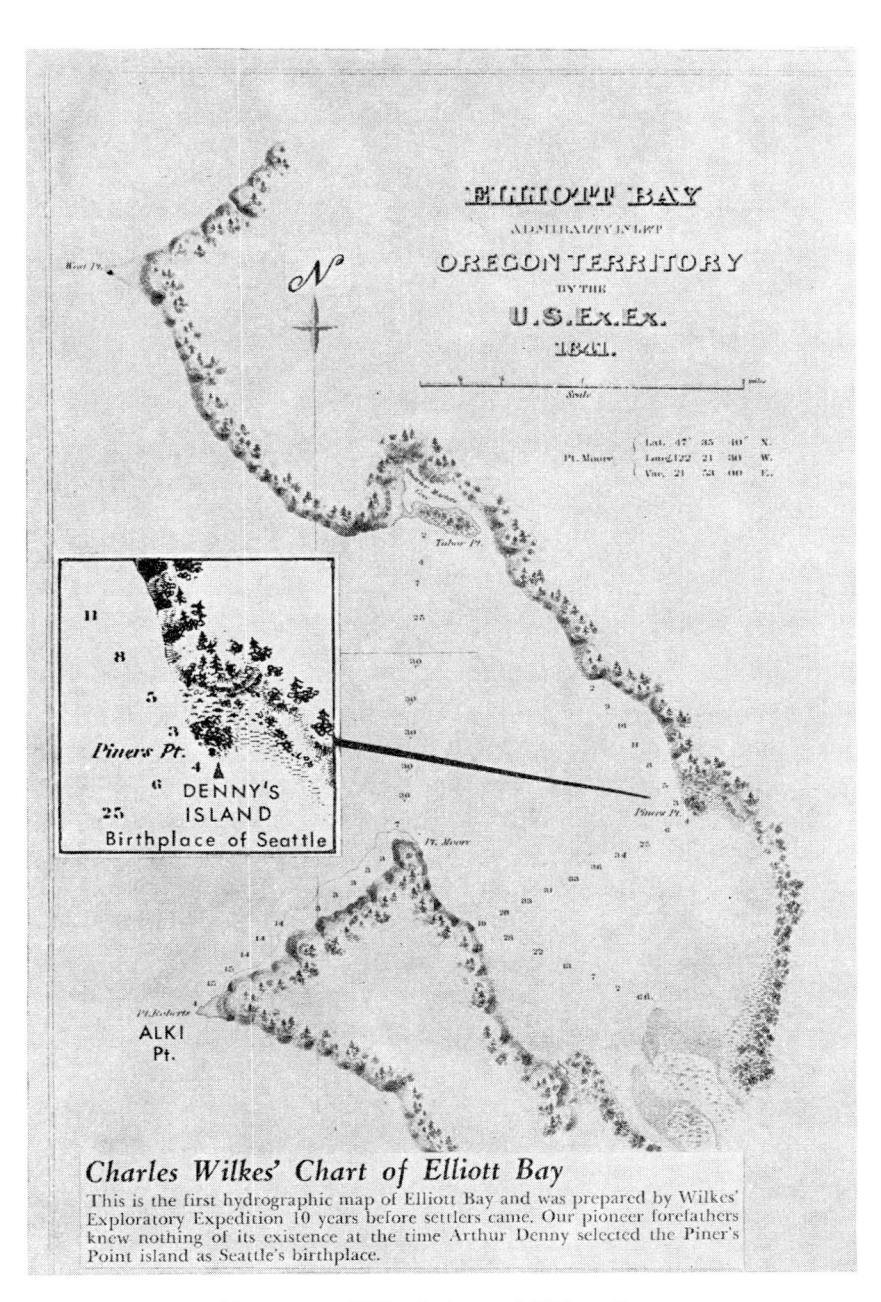

Lieutenant Wilkes' chart of Elliott Bay.

Terry knew a lost cause when he saw one and decided to drop the New York, a move that was duly noted by the Olympia *Columbian:*

"*Our enterprising friend, C.C. Terry, has made an excellent change of name for his flourishing town at the entrance to Duwamish Bay, hitherto called New York. It is henceforth to be known by the name "Alki". We never fancied the name of New York on account of its inappropriateness; but Alki we subscribe to instanter . . . it is not borrowed or stolen from any other town or city, and is in its meaning expressive unto prophesy, the interpretation of the word Alki being 'by-and-by', 'in a little while' or 'hereafter'. We must approve its application to a growing and hopeful place. Well done, friend Terry to thee and thy Alki.*"

Even that pioneer observer and historian Ezra Meeker, who visited the rival towns on Elliott Bay soon after the change of name, was impressed with the future of Alki, as he duly recorded:

"*Here (Alki) we met the irrepressible Charlie Terry, proprietor of the new townsite, who was keenly alive to the importance of adding population to his town . . . We did not stay too long in Seattle, not being favorably impressed with the place. There was not much of a town, probably twenty cabins in all . . . The lagoon presented an uninviting appearance and scent, where the process of filling with slabs and sawdust already has begun*".

But once those slabs and sawdust began appearing on the waterfront of the town across the bay, Alki was destined to languish for many years until it was engulfed by and became a scenic residential neighborhood of a metropolis called Seattle.

Home of Carson Boren; the first house built in Seattle.

Carson Boren.

CHAPTER EIGHT

Timber and Muscle

Despite his youthful optimism and boundless good nature, it must have seemed to David Denny that fate was conspiring against him in his efforts to build a home for Louisa. For six months he had devoted his energies to building homes and providing food for everybody else, and on the day his brother, with Bell and Boren, crossed the bay to stake their claims he wasn't able to go with them. He had cut himself with that slippery-handled ax again.

The three older men, wasting no time on ceremony, drove their north stake at what is now the foot of Denny Way, where the shoreline formed a small point. The south stake was driven at Piner's Point near the present site of 1st Avenue South and King Street. Arthur Denny took the center claim, Carson Boren the south and William Bell the north. A new land donation law had just been passed for "Northern Oregon" authorizing 320 acres of free land for a married couple. Like the men driving their stakes on the Elliott Bay beach, the law ignored the fact that no treaties had been signed to "extinguish" the rights of the Indians, so the land really belonged to them.

By March 17, David Denny's twentieth birthday, he had recovered sufficiently from his latest injury to cross the bay himself and stake his own claim to the north of Bell's. He wasn't of legal age yet, so he probably took it in the name of his father, John Denny, who was still farming and doing a little politicking in the Willamette Valley, or jointly with him.*

But his plans for building that honeymoon cottage were postponed again. Six weeks after his birthday, on March 23, Captain Folger brought the *Exact* back into the bay and anchored off Alki Point. He had picked up the miners who had sung "Three Blind Mice" so merrily on the way north, but they were no longer singing. While the seasick Midwesterners had recovered and established two new towns, the disillusioned miners had been finding nothing except unfriendly Indians in the Queen Charlotte Islands.

David Denny and Carson Boren were elected to return to the Willamette Valley for the rest of the livestock that had been left to winter there, and when the *Exact* left for Olympia they went with her.

A few days after their departure the big canoe of Chief Seattle glided in toward the point, its crew singing a canoe song and providing the rhythm by striking their paddles against the resonant cedar sides of the graceful craft. A well-dressed white man shared the seat of honor in the stern with the old chief.

The stranger introduced himself as David Maynard, M.D., late of Olympia, in search of a place to establish a plant for the salting and packing of salmon on a large scale for the San Francisco trade.

Doc Maynard was no teetotaler, but he was amiable and gentlemanly and he was welcomed by both the proprietors of Alki and those of the rival town across the bay, who hadn't moved to their new location yet. Charles Terry was delighted because he had recently added a cooperage shop to his various enterprises and Doc Maynard's salmon packing plant promised to be his best customer. Denny and Bell, aware of the need

---

* In 1869, the year Seattle was chartered as a town, the first plat of David's claim was filed by John and David Denny jointly.

49

for diversified industry in their embryonic city, decided to overlook the good doctor's penchant for the bottle and cordially invited him to join them in their new settlement on the east side of the bay.

According to Seattle's first historian, Frederic Grant, "*After examining the bay . . . Dr. Maynard found nothing that suited him so well as that point on the east side at the southern end of the tract set off for claims. He was readily accommodated with a site here, and the others offered to change their lines so that he might take a claim.*"

This amiable legend has been strengthened by later historians, including C.H. Hanford who, in his *Seattle and Environs,* published in 1924, wrote:

"*When Maynard decided to take a land claim and become a settler Denny, Boren and Bell had not filed in the land office notices of their claims, and to accommodate Maynard they moved their lines so as to make room for him to take a claim with the water frontage which he desired*".

A closer examination of the record indicates, however, that almost all of the waterfront that Arthur Denny and William Bell gave to Doc Maynard belonged to Carson Boren. And the gift was made while the amiable "Uncle Dobbins" was somewhere on the Cowlitz Trail with David Denny.

By April David Denny and Boren had returned from the Willamette with the stock. It had stopped raining and on that pleasant spring morning the Bell and Boren families packed their household goods into canoes and moved across the bay to set up camp while new cabins were built. Arthur and Mary Denny remained at Alki, not because they wanted to, but because they were down with the ague again, sharing the chills and fever on alternate days as they had during their stay on the Willamette.*

Interestingly enough, it was not the men of the party who chopped the first trees for homebuilding at the site of the new town, but Louisa Boren and her sister-in-law, Mrs. Carson Boren. They were among the few who weren't afflicted with chills and fever that spring, and they were impatient to settle down in a permanent home, which was understandable enough after their nomadic life of the past year.

Dr. David Maynard.

The two young women set out from Alki on a late March morning in an Indian fishing canoe and accompanied by a large dog that they hoped would protect them from the bears, cougars and wolves that roamed the forest just above the beach. They landed on Boren's claim, "made their way slowly and with difficulty through the dense undergrowth of the heavy forest" and, having reached what they considered a suitable location, "they cut with their own hands some small fir logs and laid the foundation of a cabin."

It is noteworthy that the capable Louisa had better luck with the ax than her fiance, David. She didn't cut herself.

---

* This was their last bout with this recurring malady. According to Roberta Frye Watt, "Fortunately when summer came, the famous climate that they had come west to find had its healing effect. The ague left them never to return. The climate also benefitted others of the little band, who, as we remember, were not very strong when they landed".

50

Henry Yesler.

The expedition was not without its hazards, however. March weather on Puget Sound is unpredictable and while the two determined young women were preoccupied with their building project, it took a turn for the worse. When they reached the beach they found "the wind and waves were boisterous" and the Indian canoemen nervous. So was the big dog, once he was embarked in the frail craft. As Emily Inez Denny wrote, *"One of the conditions of safe travel in a canoe is a quiet and careful demeanor, the most approved plan being to sit down in the bottom and stay there. To have a large, heavy animal squirming about, getting up and lying down frequently, must have tried their nerves severely and it must have taken good management to avert a serious catastrophe."*

By dint of skilled seamanship on the part of the Indians and determined bailing by the ladies, the canoe made it back to Alki, but the experience had "tried their nerves severely" enough that they didn't return to their building site. Their efforts were not in vain, however, for when the main party made the crossing in April the first cabin to be completed was that of Carson Boren. Bell's was a close second, and Doc Maynard's was the last of the three, although by far the most imposing. It was 26 feet long and 18 feet wide, divided between the doctor's living quarters and a drug store and general store.

When that was finished, the citizens worked together on a fourth cabin for Arthur Denny, who was still in his sickbed at Alki. They built it near the northern boundary of his waterfront atop an imposing bluff that provided an inspiring view but little else. When Arthur recovered sufficiently to move over to his new home he found it almost impossible to get to the beach, where all supplies had to be landed. Furthermore, he was unable to find water after digging a 40-foot well. Later in the summer he got David to help him build another cabin on the lower shore to the south.

By the time Arthur Denny's family made the crossing to the new town, the erstwhile New York Alki was suffering a population decline. Lee Terry, having decided once and for all that pioneering involved far too much physical labor, departed on April 18 for the real New York, never to return to the Northwest frontier. Charles Terry was still doing a brisk business with the timber-seeking shipmasters from San Francisco, but the available timber in the vicinity of his townsite was all cut down. The logging operations had to be moved across the Sound to Port Orchard. The Lows went there, he to supervise the operations and she to do the cooking for the crew. Not long afterward Low sold his interest in the town and its various enterprises to Terry and moved to Olympia.

The name for the new city was suggested by Doc Maynard for two reasons. First he thought it would be nice to honor his good friend, Chief Seattle, and second, he couldn't stand the name selected by the Territorial Legislature. Mail was being addressed to him at "Duwamps" via "Olympia, Oregon". The other settlers, having rejected the Indian name for the place, Skwudux, apparently felt that Duwamps wasn't much better. Doc's suggestion was unanimously accepted by everyone except Chief Seattle, who hadn't been consulted on the matter anyway.

It was an Indian belief that the dead awaken from their slumber when their names are mentioned by the living. Although he had been converted to the Catholic faith in his later years, the old chief hadn't forgotten a lifetime of tribal superstition and he had visions of himself turning over restlessly in his grave throughout eternity.

With everyone else taken care of, David Denny had decided that he could, in good conscience, spend some time out on his claim north of town building a cabin for Louisa and himself, but his plans were delayed again. The rest of the settlers had no sooner moved into their new homes than the brig *John Davis*, Captain George Plummer, dropped anchor off Denny's Island in search of a timber cargo for San Francisco. Everybody was running short of cash money, while sharing the determination that Terry's rival town of Alki wasn't going to get a monopoly on the area's ocean commerce.

David Denny, having honed his ax and wrapped its handle in dogfish hide to prevent its slipping, heaved a sigh and put it to work cutting and squaring timbers for the brig instead of a cabin for himself.

The *John Davis* was followed by the brig *Franklin Adams*, Captain L.M. Felker, and the two alternated in carrying building materials from Elliott Bay to San Francisco, a big wooden town that kept burning down almost as fast as it could be built up. David, along with the rest of Seattle's male population, was kept busy falling trees, trimming the smaller ones into piling and squaring the bigger ones into timbers with broadaxes. They also used mallets, frows and drawknives splitting bolts of fragrant cedar into shingles.

Doc Maynard was the only able-bodied man in town who wasn't engaged in the logging operations. He was busy operating his fish packing plant, brine-pickling the salmon brought in by his friend Chief Seattle's fishermen. During the summer he packed a thousand barrels of salmon, which he shipped to San Francisco in the two lumber brigs.

Unfortunately, Doc didn't mix his brine as strong as his drinks . . . perhaps because salt was scarcer than whiskey on the Northwest frontier . . . and all the salmon were spoiled by the time they reached their destination.

Fortunately, Doc had the foresight to sell one third of his production to Captain Plummer and another third to Captain Felker before they sailed, so he escaped total financial disaster, at least for the time being.

In addition to logging, Arthur Denny, who had been surveyor of Knox County back in Illinois, was engaged in surveying and platting the new town. Arthur handled the transit and David the staff, but still the younger brother found the time and energy during the long summer evenings to begin clearing space on his claim for a cabin and a garden. As Roberta Frye Watt wrote:

"*No one was busier nor happier than David and Louisa. In all the hard, sweaty toil, David still found time for his courting. In the long twilights and moonlit evenings, he and Louisa sat on the water's edge and planned the future . . . Seattle's first lovers. David would be twenty-one in the spring. He was clearing land for their cabin on the claim he had staked north of Mr. Bell.*

"*Perhaps the lovers felt the complete isolation of the little colony less than the others*".

Except for the occasional presence of the two San Francisco brigs in the bay, the citizens of Seattle were isolated indeed, not only from the rest of the world, but from each other. Since the claims they had staked had to be "proved up" by clearing land and building cabins, the few dwellings were necessarily widely scattered along two or three miles of shoreline on tiny plots of land hacked from the otherwise unbroken forest. The only line of communication was along the beach at low tide, or by canoe when the tide was in.

The founders of Seattle were far too busy that summer to actively recruit additional population for their town, but a few people came of their own accord. Another doctor of medicine, Henry A. Smith, paddled up from Olympia in a dugout canoe and almost continued on past the new settlement without seeing it. When he was about to give up his search he caught a glimpse of Doc Maynard's big cabin, the mercantile section of which now bore the title, "The Seattle Exchange".* Smith, then a young man of 22, took up a claim north of David Denny's where mudflats

---

* Early that fall the name of Seattle first appeared in print when Maynard advertised in the Olympia *Columbian* that his Seattle Exchange was "*now receiving direct from London and New York, via San Francisco, a general assortment of drygoods, groceries, hardware, crockery, etc., suitable for the wants of immigrants just arriving. First come, first served*".

filled a bight in the shoreline at low tide. At that location, which later became Smith's Cove, he built a cabin on the bluff, installed his mother to keep house for him, and set about clearing land for a farm. Like Doc Maynard, he had found the pioneers of Puget Sound to be disgustingly healthy and had decided that agriculture would be more profitable than the practice of medicine.

Smith was a scholar, a natural linguist and a man of letters. Like David Denny, he had respect for the Indians as human beings and took the time to learn their language. The two became warm friends as well as neighbors. It was known that an Indian trail led through the otherwise trackless forest from Elliott Bay across a Cascade Mountain pass to the land of the Yakimas, and David agreed with Smith that the doctor's cove was the natural tidewater terminus for the transcontinental railway that would some day reach Puget Sound by way of the old Indian trail across the mountains. When David filed the plat of his property, he called the thoroughfare now known as Denny Way Depot Street. More than four decades later the Great Northern Railway did reach Seattle by way of Snoqualmie Pass, and the great ocean piers that Henry Smith and David Denny had envisioned at Smith's Cove subsequently became a reality.

Another newcomer that summer was a young lawyer named George McConaha, who came with his wife aboard the *Franklin Adams* from San Francisco. McConaha built a house in the new settlement and soon after they moved in his wife gave birth to a daughter, Eugenia, who was the first white child to be born in Seattle. McConaha was, like Smith, a man of brilliant intellect and ready wit. He was an eloquent speaker and was elected the district's member of the first Territorial Legislature's Council, (The equivalent of the present State Senate) two years later after "Northern Oregon" had become Washington Territory. Although he was one of the youngest members, his fellow Council members elected him president, and it was predicted that he would some day be governor or a justice of the Territorial Supreme Court.

Like the Denny brothers, McConaha was one of the small minority of Puget Sound pioneers who didn't touch liquor, but his abstinence was based on a different reason from theirs. He was an alcoholic who had come west to start a new life, and he seemed to have succeeded, but the Legislature, then as now, was no place for an alcoholic. It was, for the most part, made up of hard-drinking frontiersmen who "took the oath of allegiance" before each session by taking hearty swigs from a jug of Blue Ruin whiskey kept behind the door of their chambers.

When the first session adjourned *sine die*, McConaha headed for the Olympia waterfront in the Indian canoe that was to take him back to Seattle, but several of his colleagues caught him, took him back to a hotel bar and forced a drink upon him. After the first one the reformed alcoholic didn't have to be forced, and it was in the early morning hours that he staggered back to his canoe. On the way down the Sound it overturned and McConaha was drowned.

If David Denny's lifelong dedication to the cause of temperance had needed strengthening, the tragic death of his friend and the plight of his widow and baby girl, would surely have provided it.

But there were also joyous events during that summer of 1852, including a visit by John Denny's wife Sarah and her small daughter Loretta, the first such reunion since the family had separated at Portland the previous autumn. An account of her journey from Olympia to Seattle was provided by E.B. Maple, who had crossed the plains to join his father at the Duwamish River settlement and traveled with Mrs. Denny, Loretta and Sarah's brother W.G. Latimer on the last leg of the journey:

"After I had been at Olympia several weeks, Dr. Maynard with four Indians and a large canoe came from Seattle to Olympia to buy goods for the Indian trade. Mrs. John Denny, mother of A.A. Denny, and Retta, her little daughter, and Mr. Latimer came from Oregon to Olympia and went on to Seattle with Dr. Maynard. On our trip down, head winds and strong tides compelled us to go ashore and camp until the wind ceased. Crossing from Vashon Island to Alki Point, we came near swamping. It kept an Indian busy bailing the water to keep the canoe from sinking. We were all glad when we got ashore. We reached Seattle about two o'clock that night and let Mrs. Denny and Mr. Latimer out at

A.A. Denny's near the beach. I went home with Dr. Maynard and stayed all night".

Certainly Sarah and little "Retta" couldn't have been more fortunate in their choice of a host for that uncomfortable and scary voyage, for the blithe spirit and vast store of human kindness of Doc Maynard was calculated to transcend such minor inconveniences as wind, waves and near swamping.

Many years later, in 1896, Latimer provided his version of the event in an interview with *Post-Intelligencer* writer Sam Crawford:

"While knocking about the beach at Olympia I met a dapper looking man who in company with a lot of Indians was loading a canoe with provisions such as flour, potatoes, beans, bacon and molasses. I entered into conversation with him, told him of my acquaintance with the Dennys and my desire to reach Seattle. He said his name was Dr. Maynard, that he lived in Seattle and that if I wished I might accompany him down the Sound, provided I had enough money or provisions. I told him I had no provisions and but 50 cts. in cash. He said that was enough and advised me to buy hardtack or sea biscuit, as that would go farther than anything else. I did as he suggested and my first journey on Puget Sound was made in an Indian canoe. We were two or three days making the journey and at night camped on the beach, Indian fashion".

But the event that changed the character and future outlook of the settlement the most took place in October and, like everyone else who wanted to get to Seattle in those days, the principle character arrived on the beach in an Indian canoe.

The man was Henry L. Yesler, short, heavily bearded and dressed in the rough clothing common to western frontiersmen, but he possessed something the other Puget Sound pioneers didn't . . . a letter of credit for $30,000 that he proposed to expend upon the construction of a steam-powered sawmill.

Yesler was born out of wedlock at Hagerstown, Maryland, in 1810 and was 42 years old when he arrived at Seattle. He had left Ohio in 1850 and wandered about the Pacific Coast for two years before he chanced to meet a sea captain in San Francisco who had just brought in a cargo of piles from Seattle. During the three weeks or so it took to cut and load the cargo, the shipmaster had spent his time exploring the area in and around Elliott Bay and come to the conclusion that the future metropolis of the Pacific Northwest would be located there.

As he explained to Yesler, the settlement was near the north-south center of Puget Sound. There was a seemingly unlimited supply of timber bordering a well protected deepwater harbor, and there was a fertile hinterland of at least a thousand acres to feed a future city. While conceding that the rival settlement of New York Alki was giving Seattle a hard run for the money at the moment, the captain predicted accurately that the winter northerly storms that sometimes swept the point would make it impossible to maintain shoreside docks or mills.

It appeared to Henry Yesler that he had found the ideal site for his steam sawmill and he wasted no time in making the journey to Puget Sound. Having made his own way in a hostile world since early childhood, he had developed a character that could perhaps most kindly be described as "crafty". He had apparently made up his mind even before he set out that he wanted to build his mill at Seattle. He paused at Olympia only long enough to procure the services of an Indian canoe and paddlers and he didn't even stop at Alki, although he told the citizens of Seattle that he had. To provide further leverage for his negotiations, he had taken the trouble to stake out a claim on the Duwamish River near the Collins-Maple-Van Asselt settlement. Yesler was shrewd enough to know that his would be the only steam sawmill on the Sound and that it was a prize any ambitious townsite would bid high for.

Doc Maynard, who lavished an almost childlike enthusiasm upon any project in which he might be engaged at the moment, was acting as a sort of one man chamber of commerce for Seattle, and he was as acutely aware as Yesler of what a steam sawmill would do for the community. He immediately took charge of convincing a seemingly reluctant Yesler that this was the ideal location for his mill.

After much cogitation and an overnight stay at the cabin of Arthur and Mary Denny, complete with the best food and entertainment that could be provided, Yesler came to

Yesler's sawmill in 1873.

the conclusion that he might be willing to locate there if the town could provide him with a few concessions.

He would like to have a piece of land at what is now First Avenue and Yesler Way upon which to build his mill and a wharf. He would also like a 450-foot wide strip of Maynard's and Boren's donation claims leading up the hill from the millsite to a ten square block area of rich timber land. And he would like the townspeople to pitch in and build the structure to house his sawmill.

Maynard cheerfully readjusted his boundaries to fit the needs of Yesler and had no difficulty in getting Carson Boren to do the same. "Uncle Dobbins" had never been interested in becoming an empire builder. All he wanted was peace and quiet and a place to hunt and fish. Unlike the other founding fathers, who had built their cabins on the beach in sight of any potential commerce, he had located his in the forest near the hunting grounds and a good trout stream. But still he wasn't getting much peace and quiet. His wife didn't like pioneering and when he came home from his hunting and fishing trips she nagged him. His brother-in-law, Arthur Denny, was always after him to clear and plat his land, and people were frequently bothering him with papers that he had to sign to move his boundary lines to accommodate somebody else.

Before long Carson Boren sold the remainder of his land for a pittance and dropped out of Seattle affairs. Doc Maynard spent the rest of his life in Seattle and died broke.

And the land they had given away made Henry Yesler more than a million dollars.

But after Yesler got his steam sawmill in operation early in 1853, it appeared to the citizens of Seattle that their investment of land and labor had been well worthwhile. A ship could be loaded in a few days instead of three weeks or more, and sawed lumber was being eagerly bought by ship captains at $35 per

---

* It is interesting to note how few of Seattle's "founding fathers" remained there long. Lee Terry returned to New York, N.Y., John Low sold out to Charles Terry and took up a new claim near Olympia. Carson Boren sold the western half of his claim to Charles Terry and Judge Edward Lander in 1855 for $500, withdrawing from the mainstream of community life, leaving only the Dennys and William Bell active in Seattle after the first five years of its founding . . . and Bell departed after the Indians attacked the town in 1856.

thousand board feet. The economic value of Seattle's timber was increased 900 percent over that of its rival communities not blessed with steam sawmills.

The previous October the projected mill had provided the first item about Seattle, other than paid advertising, in the Olympia *Columbian:*

"Huzza for Seattle! It would be folly to suppose that the mill will not prove as good as a gold mine to Mr. Yesler besides tending greatly to improve the fine town site of Seattle and the fertile country around it by attracting thither the farmer, the laborer, and the capitalist. On with improvement. We hope to hear of scores of others ere long".

The *Columbian*'s editor had made an accurate prediction.

Charles Terry did his best to keep Alki in the running. He even talked Captain William Renton into locating another steam sawmill there, but the first winter northerly knocked the pilings out from under it and the captain wasted no time in moving his enterprise across the bay to the more sheltered haven of Port Orchard. After that the shrewd Terry saw the handwriting on the wall. Although he continued to extol the virtues of Alki, he began quietly buying up land on the other side of the bay.

Yesler's mill brought prosperity to Seattle and provided jobs for anybody who wanted to work, either in the mill or in the surrounding logging operations. Roberta Frye Watt wrote:

"Every man in Seattle was needed to operate the mill. Arthur Denny, I happen to know, tended the screw that gauged the sawing of the boards and David Denny drew in the logs. Even the Indians were trained to help".

As word of Seattle's new prosperity spread, new settlers arrived and new enterprises were established around the sawmill and its big log cookhouse, which became the informal community center.

By 1853 the town had its first hotel, the Felker House, built by Captain Felker of the brig *Franklin Adams* and managed by a redoubtable lady by the name of Mary Ann Conklin, who gained a colorful place in Seattle's early history as "Mother Damnable". Doc Maynard built a blacksmith shop, although there wasn't a horse within thirty miles, and sold it to an ambitious but impecunious blacksmith for fifteen dollars. Soon afterward Thomas Mercer arrived with a team of horses and a wagon, staked a claim on Lake Union, east of David Denny's land, and began operating the first trucking company. Arthur Denny had his consignment store in operation and in the summer of 1853 it also became Seattle's first post office. A German named David Maurer opened a restaurant. The Reverend and Mrs. David Blaine arrived in town and a church was built for them, although almost everybody except Arthur and Mary Denny was too busy to attend services. Mrs. Blaine also opened the town's first school. There were no saloons, and when the first bootlegger appeared on the scene he was given short shrift by the inhabitants. The skipper of a sloop "with blue drilling sails" was observed in the illicit business of selling whiskey to the Indians on the beach north of town. Upon his next appearance, the leading citizens met him at the water's edge "and after giving him a good sound flogging took him back to the beach and bid him farewell". He did not return.

Not only was the straggling settlement taking on the semblance of a town; it had also achieved political identity. In 1852 Seattle, "New York" and the Duwamish River settlement had been lumped together by the Oregon Territorial Legislature as "Duwamps", Thurston County, Oregon Territory. Mail from "the States" was delivered to Olympia and carried down the Sound to Elliott Bay by Bob Moxlie's "canoe express" at an additional charge of twenty-five cents a letter.

By the end of 1853 Seattle had achieved the dignity of its own post office, Washington Territory had been created from Northern Oregon and King County from a portion of Thurston. The citizens of King County had participated in their first election, selecting George McConaha to represent them as councilman and Arthur Denny as representative in the first Washington Territorial Legislature, scheduled to meet at Olympia early the following year.

With the coming of local government it was necessary to formally file the plat of the town of Seattle that Arthur Denny had undertaken the previous year. The town, such as it was, clustered around Yesler's mill on the point on the claims of Arthur Denny and Doc Maynard, but Maynard's ideas of the proper way to lay out a town didn't agree with Denny's. The former Knox County surveyor laid his streets out parallel to the shoreline in a northeast-southeast direction. Doc's streets ran due north and south, so they didn't meet at Yesler's "skid road" strip of land that connected his mill with his timberlands on the bluff.

That jog in the downtown streets would create serious traffic problems for many years to come. Historians have tended to blame Maynard for the mixup, largely because of another of Arthur Denny's rare attempts at humor. In his memoirs, he wrote:

"All had gone smoothly until the time when we (Boren, Maynard and myself) were to record a joint plat of the town of Seattle, when it was found that the Doctor, who occasionally stimulated a little, had that day taken enough to cause him to feel that he was not only monarch of all he surveyed, but what Boren and I had surveyed as well. Consequently Boren and I, on the 23rd day of May, 1853, filed the first plat of the town of Seattle. When in the evening of the same day, his fever had subsided sufficiently, the Doctor filed his also".

But, as William C. Speidel has pointed out in his *Sons of the Profits*, "*the truth is that, drunk or sober, Maynard was right*".

The Donation Land Law, under which all the Seattle claims were filed, clearly specified that platted streets were to be laid out in a north-south direction.

At the moment, however, Uncle Tom Mercer's two-horse wagon constituted the only vehicular traffic in town and it would be some years before the failure of the principle streets to join one another would constitute a serious problem.

There were still no real roads connecting the isolated Puget Sound settlements and transportation was by water. A few small sailing vessels, sloops and "plungers", had begun passenger and freight service of sorts and in 1853 the region's first American steamboat, the tiny sidewheeler *Fairy*, was plying between Yesler's mill wharf and Olympia.

It had been a good year for David Denny, who less than two year earlier had constituted the entire white population of the town. Compared to his dismal surroundings of a few months before, it must have seemed to him that civilization had indeed arrived. Furthermore, his landclearing activities on his claim north of town were becoming profitable. Yesler's mill provided a ready market for the tall timber he was chopping down to make space and provide sunlight for a home and garden. As Roberta Frye Watt wrote:

"*North of town David Denny cleared the acres that are today the busy city blocks north of Denny Way. As he paused in his work he could hear the axe of his neighbor, Thomas Mercer. By ox team and by raft the timber came to the mill, from the young men logging around Salmon Bay, from the Hanford and Holgate claims, and from up the Duwamish*".

"*In spite of the hard winter of 1852-53, one of the coldest in the history of the Puget Sound country, David was able to put the finishing touches on his cabin. The acres of virgin timber on his claim had been transformed, by Yesler's mill, from a nuisance to a valuable cash crop, and his work at the mill put cash in his pockets.*"

He had been doing the work of several men during the two hard years since the little wagon train left Cherry Grove, Illinois, but in 1853 David Denny became an adult in the eyes of the law when he reached his twenty-first birthday. He felt that he had earned the right at least to claim the hand of his beloved, Louisa Boren.

When in later years the few survivors of the founding party from the *Exact* were asked how they accomplished so much in such a short time, the reply was simple and direct . . . "We did it with timber and muscle".

Surely David Denny had provided more than his share of both.

David and Louisa Denny's first home.

CHAPTER NINE

Sweetbriar Bride

David Denny had ushered in the year 1853 by making an uncomfortable canoe voyage to Olympia in search of a government official empowered to issue a marriage license. Upon his arrival he was informed that no provision had yet been made for such a document, but that Doc Maynard had been appointed by the Oregon Territorial Legislature as justice of the peace for "Duwamps" precinct, and was duly qualified to perform civil marriage ceremonies. The Reverend David Blaine didn't arrive until later in the year, so young David applied a prime axiom of the pioneers. He did the best he could with what was available.

Seattle's first wedding is probably best described by Roberta Frye Watt, who heard the details from some of those who had attended it:

"*Through all the stress of that hard winter, the romance of David and Louisa, the John Alden and Priscilla of the Seattle pilgrims, had been ripening to a happy climax. Storms on the high seas which had cut off their supplies had not interfered with their courtship, begun back in Illinois and continued across the plains. David would soon be twenty-one and now they were to be married.*

"*Louisa had many suitors. Among them was one of the skippers of the little ship Exact, who wrote to her and sent her a ring, but she sent it back saying it did not fit. When he found that she and David were engaged he said, 'You're a mighty lucky boy, Dave'.*

"*David built a little log cabin on his claim at the foot of Denny Way. It had no windows and the door was cut in half.** *As soon as it was finished, he and Louisa were married on the 23rd day of January, 1853, in Arthur Denny's cabin.*

"*The bride was as fair a one as Seattle's sun ever shone upon, with her wealth of black hair and wonderful coloring. She was dressed in soft white mull, which her own deft fingers had fashioned before she left the States.*

"*The cabin was decorated in evergreens. She and David, like two children, had gathered the greens and made the little cabin a bower. Louisa helped cook the wedding dinner of wild duck. In her own words, as she told it long afterwards:*

"'*After everything was ready, I went upstairs; or rather I climbed up a ladder to the loft where the roof was so low I couldn't stand up without bumping my head, and put on my white dress. The belt was so tight I couldn't fasten it, so I came downstairs for Mary to help me, but she was busy; so David had to fasten it for me'.*

"*The ceremony was performed by Dr. Maynard, justice of the peace, with Henry Yesler as clerk and recorder. Besides Mr. and Mrs. Arthur Denny and their children, Mr. and*

---

*This Dutch door design was popular among the early settlers for practical reasons. With window glass in short supply and very expensive, the upper half of the door could be opened during warm weather to provide both light and ventilation. The lower half provided a barrier of sorts to the always curious Indians, who would wander through a fully open door to touch as well as look at such fascinating things as the white housewife's children, dishes, utensils and food.

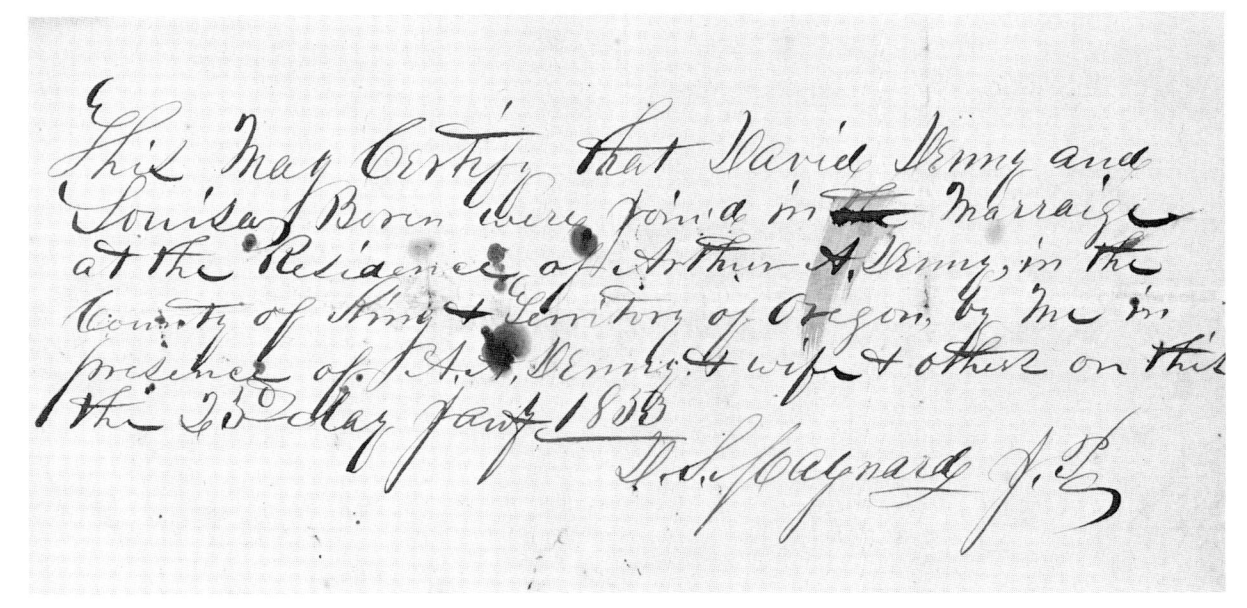

Hand-written marriage certificate of David and Louisa Denny, signed by Dr. Maynard.

Mrs. McConaha were present, also a few Indians who crowded around the door to see how the white man got his 'klootchman'.*

"After the ceremony and the wedding dinner, the bride and bridegroom went down the bluff to their canoe carrying their few wedding gifts, among which were an old hen and a rooster given them by Dr. Maynard. Chickens were scarce in those days and were considered very valuable wedding presents. Their few household goods with the hen and rooster flapping on top were packed into the canoe and they were off. The waves were heavy and the canoe lurched badly; so their wedding journey from Marion Street to Denny Way, was not without thrills, but they reached their cabin in safety.

"There they put skins and Indian mats on the floors; curtained off a pantry with blue calico; tacked on the walls some steel engravings and some pictures cut out of an old Godey's Lady's Book, that Louisa had brought across the plains; and hung the precious mirror that she had packed against her elders' wishes. On the bedstead, which was made of cedar poles with slats, they put their feather bed and gay quilts and then covered it with a hand-woven counterpane that had once graced a four-poster in the old home. On a table nearby was a brass candlestick which the bride had carried to singing school back in Illinois. The furniture was all homemade excepting a stove and a chair, which David had bought from a sailing vessel. The stove was a regulation ship's cookstove with a railing around it.

"When the room was arranged, the bride prepared the supper of salt meat and potatoes, and when the table was spread, she and David sat down to their first meal in their own home. And in that little one-roomed cabin with the earth for a floor, a bunk for a bed, a stool and a chair, and two pegs behind the door . . . one for the cap and one for the sunbonnet . . . in that little room they bowed their heads and gave thanks for their many blessings."

Although Seattle had come a long way in a remarkably short time, the home to which David Denny brought his bride in 1853 would hardly qualify as an ideal honeymoon cottage by later day standards. It was not located in the "town", but was separated from it by several miles of virtually impenetrable forest through which no trail had yet been cut. Except for the isolated cabins of Bell, Mercer

---

Klootchman or *klcochman*, in the Chinook jargon, woman.

and Dr. Smith, the region north of Arthur Denny's platted cabin was still a howling wilderness... in the literal sense of the word... inhabited only by cougars, bears, wolves and Indians, the latter generally friendly but always unpredictable.

It was a cliché of the times that "only the brave started for the West and only the strong survived". This was particularly true of the pioneer women, but Louisa Boren Denny was well fitted for survival. The independent spirit that had thwarted the edict of old John Denny and his strong-willed son Arthur to bring a mirror, Christmas presents, a white wedding gown and a brass candlestick across the plains... and the courage which had saved the women of the party from death in the Cascades of the Columbia... stood her in good stead during those first hard years.

The hen and rooster that had been the practical and kindly wedding gift of Doc Maynard came in mighty handy too, according to Mrs. Watt:

"The old hen that Dr. Maynard gave the 'newly-weds' made a nest under the doorstep, and went to sitting as soon as the nest was full of eggs. Both she and the rooster seemed to realize that there was no time to waste in this new country, for when the eggs were hatched the rooster took full charge of the chicks while the hen filled the nest again and soon came forth with a second brood.

"David was young and strong and that splendid energy that later made him a leader in city building went into providing for the new home. He supplied his table with meat from the forest... deer, elk and bear. To support his family he cut and hewed square timber and hauled it to the beach to be sent to San Francisco.

"It is fitting that the first flower garden in Seattle should have been planted by the first bride. One day in spring she planted around the cabin door a few of the precious sweetbriar seeds she had picked when she bade Pamelia Dunlap good-bye in the garden in Cherry Grove. The sweetbriar grew and scattered over the town, and the old settlers called Louisa Denny 'the sweetbriar bride'.

"This sweetbriar continued to grow at the foot of Denny Way until a short time ago... seventy-seven years after the seeds were planted (1931)... when the last trace of it was uprooted by the jaws of the steam shovel.

"I always think of the 'sweetbriar bride' when I read of a beautiful wedding. The wedding may be more elaborate. The gifts more costly, but, I am sure, none is happier than was Seattle's first bride. Then in the springtime, when thoughts of gardening are in the air, I try to picture that first little garden about the cabin door".

Years later, in 1928, when Seattle's civic auditorium (now rebuilt as an opera house) was built on David Denny's old claim, a few of the seeds from Louisa Denny's sweetbriar vines were included among the artifacts sealed up in the cornerstone.

Emily Inez Denny's account of her parents' early life in their isolated claim, as remembered by her mother in later years, provides a vivid picture:

"Stern realities confronted them; a part of the time they were out of flour and had no bread for days; they bought fish of the Indians, which, together with game from the forest, brought down by the rifle of the pioneer, made existence possible.

"And then, too, the pioneer housewife soon became a shrewd searcher for indigenous articles of food. Among these were nettle greens gathered in the woods. In their season the native berries were very acceptable; the salmon-berry ripening early in June; dewberries and red and black huckleberries were plentiful in July and August.

"The first meal partaken of in this cabin consisted of salt meat from a ship's stores and potatoes. They afterward learned to make a whole meal of a medium sized salmon with potatoes, the fragments remaining not worth mentioning.

"The furniture of their cabin was meager, a few chairs from a ship, a bedstead made of fir poles and a ship's stove were the principle articles. One window without glass but closed by a wooden shutter with the open upper half-door served to light it in the daytime, while the glimmer of a dogfish-oil lamp was the illumination at night".

The marriage of David and Louisa was the culmination of the westward drive of two pioneer families, for Louisa Boren was a direct descendant of Elder William Brewster, a leader of the *Mayflower* party that had

One of Louisa Denny's flower gardens.

crossed the Atlantic to the New World even before the Ulster Scot Dennys.

In her later years Louisa Denny told her children and grandchildren stories of her early married life with David in their wilderness cabin. Their memories of her eye witness accounts are a part of Pacific Northwest history, both written and oral, vividly portraying the fear and uncertainty that were faced every day and every night by the first pioneer women.

With David toiling from dawn to dark felling timber to clear their claim and provide cash income, Louisa was usually alone . . . in later years with a growing family of small children . . . from early morning until late at night, always anxiously awaiting the safe return of her husband and, as the hostility of many of the Indians increased, fearful for her own safety and that of the children. The vast forest that surrounded the cabin was the hunting ground of cougar, bear and wolves, as unseen but as ever present as the wandering bands of Indians. The children were never allowed to wander far from the cabin and were taught to blow out the candles if they heard any unusual sound after dark.

She vividly recalled how the profound silence of the nighttime forest was "filled with a thousand sounds many times magnified". In that stillness the falling of a leaf, the sudden cry of a night bird, or the soft tread of a wild animal could easily become the threat of creeping Indians. In fact, the hooting of owls, the calls of birds and the cries of wild animals were used by the Indians to signal each other.

And often, in the early morning darkness, they were awakened by the unmistakable and savage sounds of the Indians themselves . . . their eerie chanting as they sought to drive away evil spirits, the shrill wailing of the women for the dead and sometimes, most frightening of all, the hairlifting sound of the Duwamish war cry, described by Louisa as "a loud, harsh bawl that could strike terror to the most courageous heart".

Louisa Denny was a strong woman, physically as well as spiritually, better equipped than most to survive the loneliness, the fears and the continuing hardships of life on the last frontier, but she was not entirely immune to human weakness.

She told of one time during those early years when she had become so ill that she hadn't been able to get up in the morning to prepare breakfast. After making her as comfortable as possible, David took ax and rifle and went to work, promising to return early to the cabin.

At their nearest neighbors, the Bells, who lived a mile to the south, William Bell presented his wife with a half dozen fresh pheasant eggs that he had found in the course of an early morning stroll. Knowing that Louisa hadn't been well, Mrs. Bell decided to take the eggs, considered a great delicacy by the pioneers, to her ailing friend. The tide was low, so she was able to walk along the beach to the Denny cabin. She poached the eggs and prevailed upon Louisa to eat a little. Then she sat down to engage in that cherished pastime of the lonely pioneer women, "visiting".

As the two friends talked, two strange Indians came furtively out of the forest and stared insolently at the two white women over the open half-door. The women ignored them and after some gutteral whispering, the two braves departed as silently as they had come.

Afterward friendly Indians told David that the wandering Klikitats who had approached the cabin had intended to murder Louisa and rob the isolated home, but seeing Mrs. Bell there, they feared the husbands might also be nearby. David's marksmanship was legendary among the Indians and they decided to let discretion be the better part of valor.

The story, although it had a happy ending, illustrates how completely the pioneer women were at the mercy of the Indians when their husbands were away hunting or cutting timber.

In addition to the endless tasks involved in keeping a growing family fed, clothed and clean under primitive frontier conditions, Louisa Denny found time to plant an old-fashioned flower garden around the cabin in the forest. Her daughter tells us in *Blazing the Trail*, that wherever her mother made her home, even for a brief period, she planted a garden of old-fashioned flowers. Roses and hollyhocks, pansies and tiger lilies, honeysuckle and sweet William, and mignonette shared the sunlight and rain with the legendary sweetbriar in flower beds outlined with white stones from the beach. Her brother Carson, more interested in Louisa's laying out of flower gardens than his fellow founder's efforts to lay out a city, brought back pink mission rose bushes from Steilacoom to add to her collection.

In December, 1853, a daughter, Emily Inez, was born to David and Louisa Denny at their wilderness cabin.

She was the only one of their eight children born there. The second was destined to first draw the breath of life amid far less tranquil surroundings.

John Denny in his later years.

CHAPTER TEN

Indian War

Most of the earliest settlers in the Puget Sound country made it a practice to treat the Indians fairly and kindly, for practical as well as humanitarian reasons. The first Washington Territorial Census of 1853 showed a total white population of only about 170 white men, women and children in all of King County, while the confederated tribes of Chief Seattle numbered some four thousand. It would obviously have been foolish to deliberately antagonize the Indians who outnumbered the white settlers so overwhelmingly.

Some, like Luther Collins of the Duwamish River settlement, adhered to the code grudgingly while making no secret of his contempt for the "dirty Siwashes", but a majority of the true pioneers made real and lasting friendships among the generally good-natured Sound Indians.

David Denny was the first to master the Duwamish tongue and thereafter his circle of Indian friends grew steadily. His pretty wife Louisa was a general favorite among them and stern Arthur Denny had been viewed with deep respect since he had forthrightly broken up a confrontation of rival Indian bands during the early days on Alki Point.

There was a genuine comradeship between Doc Maynard and old Seattle that lasted as long as the old chief lived, and Henry Yesler was able to parley successfully with the even potentially hostile tribes. Carson Boren, one of the few frontiersmen who did not covet the Indians' land, had become, like the Indians, a wanderer in the forest, a dreamer and a hunter, and they viewed him as almost one of themselves.

But as more settlers arrived in 1853, 1854 and 1855, pushing further into the ancient hunting grounds of the Indians, tensions mounted. Not all the newcomers observed the earlier code of decency toward the Indians. Some used whiskey to rob them of reason and possessions and to debauch their women. Some offered them jobs and refused to pay them when the work was done, and there were some who viewed the Indians as "varmints" who should be hunted and destroyed like the wolves and cougars of the forest.

During the summer of 1853, a Duwamish Indian known as Masachie (Bad) Jim, in a drunken rage brought on by white man's whiskey, killed his "klootchman". Such intratribal crimes had, in the past, been handled by Chief Seattle and the tribal elders, but this time a group of Seattle Indian-haters, no doubt stimulated by the same beverage that had triggered the killing in the first place, decided to take the law into their own hands. They dragged Masachie Jim to the edge of town and hanged him from a tree limb that evening.

The lynching was not just a stupid and lawless thing to do; it was the first of a series of events that would open the floodgates of Indian resentment and lead to war.

Another murder occurred soon after the lynching, but the white citizens of Seattle didn't learn about it until a year later. A man believed to have been a seaman from one of the San Francisco sailing vessels, was waylaid, murdered and robbed by a band of Indians in the forest near Lake Union. The body was concealed and his money and possessions divided, but the crime soon became common knowledge among all the Indians of the area, who were much troubled. They believed that an evil spirit hovered over the scene of the murder and would cast an evil spell upon them all.

It was David Denny, with his thorough knowledge of the tribal language, who discovered their secret, probably to the relief of those who had not participated in the killing.

As he was passing an Indian hut on his way from working a shift at Yesler's mill he heard a loud argument going on inside and went to investigate. When he got closer he heard one Indian accuse another of having killed a white man. Although he was alone and unarmed, he strode into their midst and demanded an explanation.

The Indians were surprised and frightened, and at first lapsed into a sullen silence, but since David was their friend and they trusted him, they finally agreed to let Hu-hu-batesute, known to the white people as Salmon Bay Curley, tell him what had happened.

Organized government and justice had come to Seattle since the lynching of the previous year; (David had been one of the election judges who certified the election of Carson Boren as Sheriff of King County), so he felt safe in reporting what he had learned to the other settlers.

A search party was quickly formed, consisting of David Denny, Maynard, Bell, Boren and Seattle's first photographer, a daguerreotypist named E. A. Clark who subscribed to the theory that the only good Indian was a dead one. Salmon Bay Curley guided them to the scene of the crime, where Doc Maynard gathered the fragments of the victim's skull into a handkerchief to serve as *corpus dilecti*, along with two pairs of spectacles, "one gold-rimmed, the other steel-rimmed", which had been left by the Indians.

Four Indians were arrested for the murder and a justice court trial was held in the Felker House. An Indian named Klap-ke-lachi Jim testified positively against two of the accused and implicated the others. The first two were found guilty, led from the improvised courtroom and summarily hanged from a conveniently leaning stump.

One of the other accused Indians, called Old Petawow, had broken his leg and was carried into court by two of his friends. It was decided that there wasn't sufficient evidence to convict him and he was released, but the fourth defendant, a young brave, was ordered held by Sheriff Boren "on suspicion". Since the citizens of Seattle hadn't gotten around to building a jail, Boren locked the prisoner in a room in his own house.

Their appetite for hanging having been whetted, a mob headed by Clark decided to lynch Boren's prisoner. After sharing their bottles with some seamen from a ship anchored in the harbor, the members of the mob borrowed a block and tackle from them, set up a tripod of spars awaiting shipment from Yesler's wharf, and thus improvised a suitable gallows.

Boren's reputation as a crack shot and an advocate of equal justice for Indians was well known, so a diversionary move was decided upon to get him out of range. One of the drifters in the crowd was dispatched to the sheriff's house on the pretext that he wanted to buy some barrels that had been left in Boren's care by a cooper and stacked on the beach some distance from his house.

The unsuspecting sheriff accompanied the visitor to the beach where the stranger engaged him in a long and rambling conversation regarding barrels, the best recipes for brine and economics of salmon-packing. At length, probably convinced that his coconspirators had had plenty of time to break the "jail", and not wanting to miss the lynching, the barrel fancier said, "maybe we'd better get back. The boys are threatening mischief".

Thus rudely brought back to reality, Sheriff Boren started up the beach at a dead run. He arrived at the improvised scaffold just in time. The young Indian had the noose about his neck, Clark was officiating as hangman and Luther Collins was loudly proclaiming that this was the only way to deal with the murdering Siwash. Four seamen from the lumber brig were holding the rope awaiting Clark's order to pull.

The more law abiding citizens had long since left for their homes and the usually gentle and easy-going "Uncle Dobbins" faced the mob alone. He may have lacked ambition, but Carson Boren didn't lack courage.

"Drop that rope, you rascals!", he bellowed, "You have no right to hang him. He'll be tried at the next term of court".

Abashed, the sailors dropped the rope, Boren removed the noose from around the neck of the stoical young Indian, and the mob dispersed. The Indian was sent to the brick jail at Steilacoom and was subsequently tried and found innocent.

Between the lynching of Masachie Joe, the murder of the itinerant traveler on the shores of Lake Union and the trial and mob execution of his convicted killers, the citizens of Seattle had received further proof of growing Indian hostility. In March of 1854 William Young, the engineer at Captain Renton's sawmill, then located at Alki, made a trip to Whidbey Island in an Indian canoe and failed to return. Suspecting that he had met with foul play, Thomas Russell, the deputy sheriff at Alki, led a posse north to arrest the Indian canoemen who were suspected. The posse caught up with the Indians at Holmes Harbor and a pitched battle ensued. Several of the Indians were killed and all the posse members wounded. One of them, Dr. W. G. Cherry, died soon after being brought to Seattle. Funeral services were conducted by the Reverend David Blaine and he was buried near the beach on Doc Maynard's point.

After the services a "company of volunteers" was formed to immediately go out and shoot any Indians they might come upon, but calmer heads prevailed and the citizens compromised by drawing up a resolution urging Territorial Governor Isaac I. Stevens to establish a Territorial Militia for the protection of the settlers.

Thus it was that the vicious circle of hatred and intolerance spread like the waves from a rock flung carelessly into the Sound.

Even David and Louisa, good friends of the Indians though they were, were not spared the threat of violence to come. When little Emily Inez was older her mother told her of some of these incidents and, later still, she told of them in her book:

"Dr. Choush, an Indian medicine man, came along one day in a state of ill-suppressed fury. He had just returned from a Government 'potlatch'* at the Tulalip agency. In relating how they were cheated he said that the Indians were presented with strips of blankets which had been torn into narrow pieces about six to eight inches wide, and a little bit of thread and a needle or two. The Indians thereupon traded among themselves and pieced the strips together.

"He was naturally angry and said menacingly that the white people were few, their doors were thin and the Indians could easily break them in and kill the 'Bostons'. All this could not have been very reassuring to the inmates of the cabin; however they were uniformly kind to the natives and had many friends among them".

Later, shortly before the outbreak of organized hostility by the Indians, according to Miss Denny, *"A troop of Indians visited this cabin and their bearing was so haughty that Mrs. Denny felt very anxious. When they demanded 'Klosh mika potlatch wapatoes' (Give us some potatoes) she hurried out herself to dig them as quickly as possible that they might have no excuse for displeasure, and was much relieved when they took their departure. One Indian remained behind a long time but talked very little. It was supposed that he thought of warning them of the intended attack on the white settlement but was afraid to do so because of the enmity against him that might follow among his own people".*

The Indians' opinion of white man's justice could hardly have been heightened when, in October, 1854, King County's first grand jury convened at the Felker House to consider the lynching of Masachie Jim and the two Indians convicted of the Lake Union murder.

The handful of white settlers in the area constituted a tight-knit community of friends and neighbors. They had shared with each other in times of scarcity, worked together to clear the timber and build homes, cared for each other in illness and celebrated together on such festive occasions as Christmas and the Fourth of July.

---

*Potlatch, described in George C. Shaw's *Chinook Jargon and How to Use It* (1909) as: "The greatest institution of the Indian . . . From far and near assembled the invited guests and tribes and with feasting, singing, chanting, and dancing, the bounteous collection was distributed; a chief was made penniless, the wealth of a lifetime was dissipated in an hour, but his head was ever after crowned with the glory of a satisfied ambition; he had won the honor and reverence of his people. It was a beautiful custom; beautiful in the eyes of the natives of high or low degree, confined to no particular tribe, but to be met with everywhere along the coast".

Agents of the federal government adopted the traditional gift-giving as a preliminary to the treaty-making which would extinguish the claims of the Indians to their lands. The distribution of such paltry items as torn blankets, "jewsharps" and blackstrap molasses had the opposite of the desired effect, however. Some of the Indians believed these constituted their entire payment, and all scorned the white man's parsimony.

The Rev. Daniel Bagley.

Dexter Horton.

Even men like David Denny and Doc Maynard, compassionate friends of the Indians though they were, in the end found it impossible to sacrifice their friends and neighbors to the principle of abstract justice.

Charles Terry, now actively engaged in promoting his town lots on what had been Carson Boren's claim, was foreman of the 20-man grand jury. David and Arthur Denny were members of the trial jury impaneled to act upon any indictments handed down by the grand jury. Another jury member was Dexter Horton, a young man who had crossed the plains with Thomas Mercer and Daniel Bagley and later came to Seattle penniless and, like the earlier arrivals, sick with the ague. He had since progressed to a partnership with Arthur Denny and David Phillips in the mercantile establishment of Horton, Denny & Phillips and would, in later years, become Seattle's first and most successful banker.

When the grand jury, after spending as much time as possible deliberating such lesser matters as the illegal dumping of ballast by shipmasters and the illegal sale of whiskey to Indians, got down to the lynchings there was considerable excitement at that community gathering place, Yesler's cookhouse. A hat was passed to raise money for "the smartest lawyers in the territory" to defend any fellow citizens who might be indicted. The subscription list was headed by Doc Maynard, who gave $150.

The grand jury proceedings had distinct comic opera overtones that began when the jurors found that one of their fellow members, one William Heebner, was accused of complicity in the hanging of the Indians. Charles Terry adroitly solved this legal contretemps by excusing Mr. Heebner long enough to indict him, after which he returned to his seat on the panel.

Two other prominent settlers, David Maurer and Luther Collins, the latter a King County commissioner, were also indicted and the cases turned over to the trial jury. Maurer, whom historian Thomas Prosch described as a "simple-minded Dutchman," was tried first. When asked whether he was entering a plea of guilty or not guilty he replied, "I suppose I ish guilty, Shudge."

Terry, erstwhile foreman of the grand jury, leaned over and in a loud whisper told

Dr. Henry A. Smith.

Gov. Isaac I. Stevens.

Maurer, "*Not* guilty, you fool; say not guilty." Maurer quickly changed his plea and a declaration of innocence was entered in the record. Both Maurer and Heebner were subsequently acquitted, after which prosecuting attorneys Elwood Evans and Frank Clark threw up their hands and asked for the dismissal of the charges against Collins.

Although the white settlers were to reap a whirlwind of death and destruction as the result of such one-sided justice, Mother Damnable, as proprietor of the Felker House, reaped a tidy profit from the court session. She submitted a bill listing $25 for the use of her parlor as a court room, $10 for jurors' rooms, $4.00 for the use of her furniture and $66 for jurors' meals. When Clark, the Territorial prosecutor, ventured the opinion that the bill was "a little steep" and requested a receipt, the terrible tempered lady, who couldn't read or write and didn't like the prosecutor anyway, gathered an apron full of stove wood and drove Clark from the premises by throwing the sticks at him with dreadful accuracy.

The final spark that ignited the flames of inter-racial warfare in the Puget Sound country was struck by Washington Territory's new governor, Isaac Stevens who, late in 1854, began a whirlwind round of treaty-making that carried him from Puget Sound to the Rocky Mountains. The first treaty was made at Medicine Creek on the Nisqually River delta near Olympia the day after Christmas. By the terms of this treaty with the Nisqually, Puyallup, Steilacoom, Squaxin and other tribes, they were to give up their title to land comprising half of King County and all of what is now Thurston, Pierce and Mason Counties. In return they were to receive the usual trinkets, three small reservation areas and $32,000 in cash and other benefits to be paid over a period of years.

The reservation assigned to the largest tribe, the Nisqually, was a gravelly hilltop providing only about four acres per family. The Nisqually were farmers and horse-breeders as well as fishermen and the arid reservation assigned to them would support neither crops nor stock.

Leschi, the most influential of the Nisqually leaders, bitterly protested the injustice of the treaty, convinced that it would be better to die in battle than to slowly starve to death on an untenable reservation. When word of his defiance reached Olympia, Territorial Secretary Charles Mason dispatched a company of volunteer militia to take him into custody.

Leschi who, like Seattle, had welcomed the first white settlers to his land, was helping his brother, Quiemuth, plow his farm when word of his planned arrest reached him. Leaving the plow of peace to rust in its furrow, Leschi and Quiemuth took their weapons and fastest horses and escaped, gathering armed warriors to join forces with the Eastern Washington Indians who had already chosen the path of war.

But to the citizens of Seattle, the year 1855 seemed by far the best in the brief history of their town. Coal had been discovered east of Lake Washington and Captain William Webster had brought the little side-wheel steamer *Water Lily* up from San Francisco to tow loaded coal barges across the lake. Coal as well as timber was being shipped to San Francisco. New settlers continued to arrive, assured of work in the mill, which hummed day and night employing two twelve-hour shifts. The first rude cabins were giving way to neatly painted houses of finished lumber, surrounded by gardens and neat picket fences. Four general stores were doing a flourishing business on "Commercial Street" near the mill and one of them, Plummer & Chase's, had secured licenses to operate a bar and "bowling salloon." It had also become the post office and, with the legal availability of "spiritous liquors," the successor to Yesler's cookhouse as the favorite gathering place for the town's male population (with the exception, of course, of David and Arthur Denny and the Reverend Blaine).*

Historians, gifted with the wisdom of hindsight, have sometimes expressed surprise that the Elliott Bay settlers failed to comprehend the imminence of violence and death, but they were young and healthy and full of hope. Prosperity had come at last and they were beginning to reap the fruits of their hardships and toil. The Indian troubles of the turbulent summer of 1854, most of them were convinced, had been ended by the treaties of Governor Stevens.

Most of the settlers were indeed convinced that Steven's treaties, which were at least a major factor in bringing Indian hostility to a head, would settle all their problems, an idea fostered by the Olympia *Pioneer and Democrat* (successor to the *Columbian*), which on December 30, 1854, had commented blandly that *"On Tuesday, the 26th of this month, a treaty was made with several Indian tribes at the head of the Sound whereby they relinquished all their lands . . . Great pains were taken to express the provisions of the treaty, and the Indians were entirely satisfied."*

This feeling of false security was expressed by the Reverend Blaine's wife Catherine in one of her letters:

"Our governor has been employed some weeks past in treating with the Indians on the Sound . . . They seem entirely satisfied with the treaty as far as I can learn . . . I think we shall apprehend no more trouble from them."

Mrs. Blaine had apparently been reading the *Pioneer and Democrat* instead of talking to the Indians.*

David Denny was one Seattleite who *had* been talking to the Indians and listening to

---

*Neither of the Denny brothers ever budged an inch when it came to their principles, with the single exception of the agonizing decision as jurors not to vote for conviction of their friends and neighbors in the illegal hanging of the three Indian murderers. Both took pride in the fact that they "had never kept a saloon" and, although whiskey was a major item of merchandise . . . and a profitable one . . . Arthur's high regard for a dollar didn't overcome his strong feelings about the evils of drink. During his days as a storekeeper "spiritous liquors" were never included in his stock.

---

*Independent minded Louisa Denny formed her own opinion of Stevens. Nearly fifty years later she told her grandson, Victor Denny, Jr., that she considered the territorial governor to be incompetent and his handling of the Indian situation "a complete disaster".

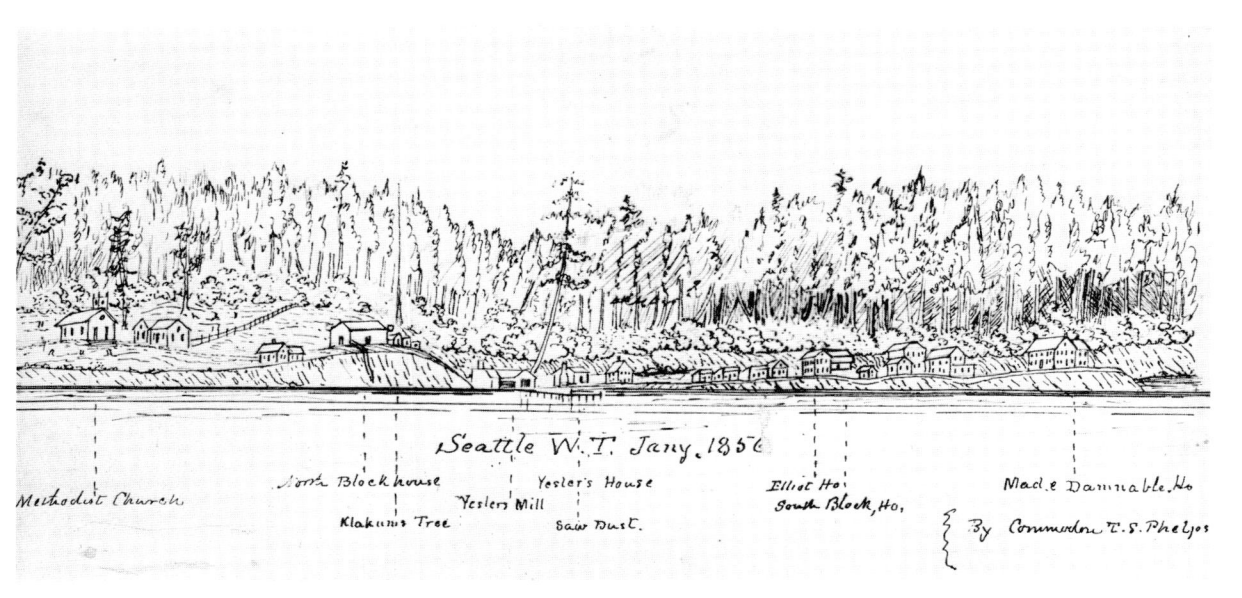

Sketch of Seattle at the time of the battle, drawn by Lt. Thomas S. Phelp.

them as well. His knowledge of their language and the high regard in which he and Louisa were held made him among the first to realize that serious trouble was brewing. He had worked hard for his home and he was not easily frightened, but the repeated warnings of his Indian friends could not be ignored. His instinct might be to stand and defend his isolated claim against all comers, but practical considerations made that impossible. He must work to support his family and while he was away his wife and baby daughter were defenseless. Sadly he and Louisa packed their household treasures, nailed shut the door of their honeymoon cabin and moved into a small house near Arthur Denny's home in the center of the village of 40 buildings and 250 people.

The killing had started east of the Cascade Mountains when prospectors, stampeding toward a new gold rush on the Colville River, violated the tribal hunting grounds of the Yakimas and were gunned down from ambush. Early in the summer of 1855 two men named Fanjoy and Eaton left Seattle for the supposed gold fields and were not heard of again. Later that summer Arthur Denny, Judge Lander and Hillory Butler, a Virginian who had arrived at Seattle in 1853, left to inspect the recently built wagon road over the Cascade Mountains. They had gotten only a few miles east of town and were camped on the Black River when a messenger arrived by canoe to take them back as quickly as possible.

Soon after their departure, three prospectors had staggered into Seattle half starved and completely exhausted after making their way over the mountain pass, hiding by day and traveling by night. They were the survivors of a party of five that had left Seattle a few weeks after the departure of Fanjoy and Eaton. They had reached the Yakima Valley when two of the party, walking ahead of the others, were shot down by the Indians.

There could be no doubt about it now. The Indian War had begun and the road surveying party was walking into it. David Denny and Carson Boren wasted no time in dispatching the messenger to recall them.

The war came closer to home three weeks later, as described by Roberta Frye Watt:

"All accounts of Seattle's part in the Indian War begin with the experience of Allen L. Porter of White River. Mr. Porter had been one of the Biles train that had cut its way through the Naches Pass in the summer of

'53. By this time he had cleared his land so that his ranch was beginning to repay him for his labor.

"When he heard the terrifying word that the Yakimas had murdered two Seattle men on their way to the gold fields and that his neighbors down the valley, Fanjoy and Eaton, had doubtless met the same fate, he began to fear for his own safety since he was alone in the upper valley. Not wishing to abandon his ranch he took the precaution of sleeping outside in the bushes, as the Indians frequently attacked under the cover of darkness. He had done this several times, when, on the night of September 27, 1855, he saw some men at his house. Thinking they were white men needing shelter he hurried forward, and was nearly on them when he discovered that they were Indians. It did not take him long to realize that they had come to murder him. Not finding him they attacked his house.

"Then, like another Paul Revere, he hurried down the river, his steed a swift canoe, warning the settlers as he fled toward Seattle. All of them soon followed and came into the village, frightened refugees, forced to leave their homes and gardens, all the fruit of their toil to the Indians. It was sickening news to the settlers of Seattle."

The arrival of Porter and the rest of the panic-stricken White River settlers brought the reality of Indian hostility close to home for the citizens of Seattle. David Denny had recently cut a large consignment of timber, which was rafted on the beach awaiting the arrival of a ship for San Francisco. The timbers represented weeks of hard labor and several hundred dollars in badly needed cash money, but as always, the welfare of the community came first. On the next high tide the logs were floated to the village waterfront and dragged up the hill to the foot of Cherry Street where construction was begun on a blockhouse "where all might retreat in case of an attack".

David was also active in the formation of a company of volunteers to man the blockhouse and defend the town if need be. Christopher C. Hewitt, a frontier lawyer who was later appointed by President Lincoln as chief justice of the Territorial Supreme Court, was elected captain; David Denny was one of the two noncommissioned officers. The Seattle volunteer company was duly enrolled as a unit of the Territorial militia to serve for a

U.S. sloop of war Decatur.

period of three months. Although there were about eighty officers and men in its muster roll, they possessed only about half that number of serviceable firearms. A number of the volunteers were issued rusty muskets that couldn't be fired but would, it was hoped impress the Indians who watched the amateur soldiers at drill.

Despite these efforts at defense, the prospect was not a cheerful one. As Roberta Frye Watt wrote: *"They were perilously unguarded, back of them the forest that might hide an Indian horde, and in front of them the Bay. And they were few in number . . . only a little over two hundred souls in all . . . compared with thousands of Indians. The situation was indeed serious".*

It was at this point, with the blockhouse half finished and the volunteers, rugged individualists all, arguing over military tactics and who should have the workable weapons, that history repeated itself.

During the dreary winter of 1851 the sails of the brig *Leonesa*, rounding West Point and entering Elliott Bay, had brought a degree of economic security to the discouraged settlers. On the pleasant Indian summer day of October 4, 1855, another ship, standing in close-hauled around the point, brought a degree of military security to the beleaguered settlement. It was the United States sloop of war *Decatur*, Captain Isaac S. Sterrett, which backed her yards off Yesler's wharf and drop-

THOMAS S. PHELPS

Leschi of the Nisquallies.

ped her anchor in the deep water close off shore.

The *Decatur* had been ordered from Honolulu to "cruise on the coast of Oregon and California for the protection of settlers". Captain Sterrett had, fortunately for the citizens of Seattle, interpreted his orders rather broadly and set his course for Puget Sound. Arriving at Port Townsend in mid-July, he learned of the increasing hostility of the Indians in Washington Territory, but since his ship was short of ammunition and supplies he took her down the coast to the San Francisco Navy Yard for replenishment before taking up station on the Sound.

Governor Stevens was far away in the Bitter Root country making more treaties with the Indians and the territorial secretary, twenty-nine-year-old Charles Mason was acting governor. Having heard of the White River panic, he borrowed a detachment of soldiers from the Army post at Fort Steilacoom and set out to investigate. The local Indians sized up the well armed, well disciplined regulars and assured Mason that they were very fond of the "Boston" people, that they had never attacked anybody's house and that the settlers had been frightened by a false alarm.

Young Mason arrived at Seattle thoroughly convinced that the White River settlers were the victims of mass hysteria. He assured them that they were in no danger and told them to return to their farms. Urged on by the need to tend their crops, they followed his advice, found their homes undisturbed and the Indians seemingly friendly, and concluded, as had Mason, that Porter's alarm had been false.

Mason also boarded the *Decatur* and told Captain Sterrett that the whole affair had been staged by the civic leaders of Seattle to keep his ship in the harbor and make a profit on the sale of whiskey and other supplies essential to the Navy. The captain stormed ashore and into Arthur Denny's store, denouncing him and his fellow townspeople as "a lot of cowards, squatters and land sharks", and informing him that the *Decatur* was going to hoist anchor and depart immediately. Arthur, who had just been elected to his third term in the Territorial Legislature, had acquired some of his father's skill in the art of politics. He kept his temper and presented such cogent arguments that Captain Sterrett became, if not convinced, confused. He decided to stay a while and find out for himself who was right.

Even a number of the settlers agreed with Mason's false alarm theory. They could see no reason to sweat over the heavy timbers on the blockhouse project when the sloop of war lay in the bay with its gunports open and a crew of trained sailors and marines on deck who were being paid to protect them. Soon there were more scoffers making rude jokes than workers at the construction site. When Louisa Denny, bringing David his lunch, heard one of the cynical settlers poking fun at her husband she promptly put him in his place with the tart observation that "people laughed at Noah when he built the ark".

There appear to have been warnings enough from friendly Indians to convince at least the earlier settlers that an attack was coming. Salmon Bay Curley convinced the Hanford family, living on a claim to the south of the village, that they should move to the security of the blockhouse. Yarkekman Jim, an Indian who often worked for the Dennys and was known as "Denny Jim", gained the full confidence of the *Decatur*'s officers, providing them with accurate information regarding the plans of the hostile chiefs. Louisa Denny said in later years that Chief Seattle, before moving with his tribe to a reservation established across the Sound by Maynard, had come to their cabin to warn them solemnly in the Duwamish tongue that war was surely coming.

Despite the warnings and rumors, the village seemed peaceful enough on the bright Sunday evening of October 28 . . . until a canoe came slashing across the bay from the mouth of the Duwamish carrying a half dozen of the White River settlers who had returned to their farms less than two weeks before. They had been shot at by Indians and, as they ran for the river, they had heard more gunfire and screams from further up the valley.

The next morning another canoe arrived from upriver, paddled by an Indian known as "Indian Dave" and carrying three small white children huddled in the bottom. The oldest of them, six-year-old John King, told the settlers enough to convince them that a savage massacre had taken place in the White River Valley.

Thomas Phelps, a lieutenant on the *Decatur* wrote the only contemporary published account of what came to be known as

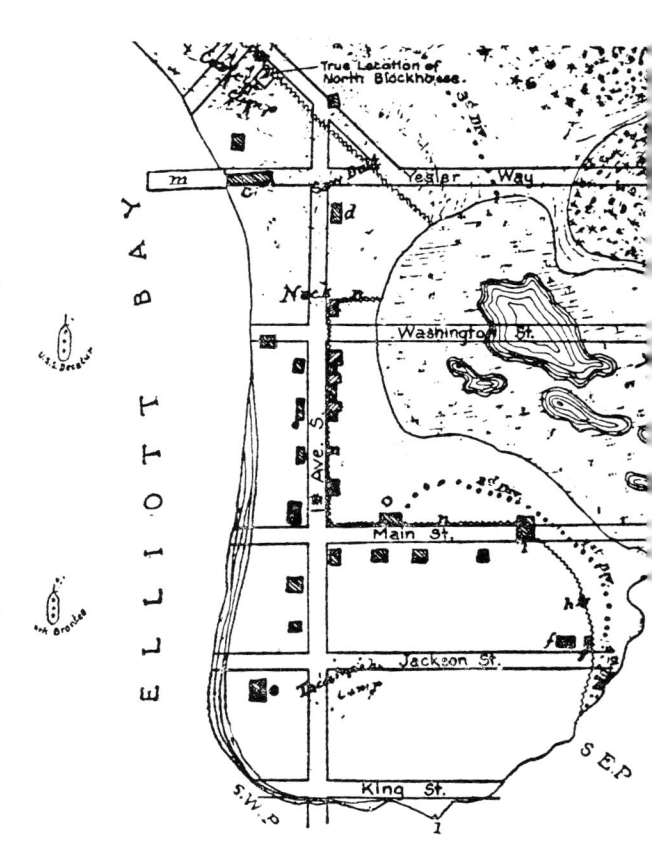

Phelps' map of Seattle, 1856.

the Battle of Seattle. In it he was extravagant in his charges of cowardice and insubordination against the Seattle volunteer company. Insubordinate they were, at least by regular Navy standards, for they were rugged frontier types with minds of their own and a number of them became self-made millionaires in later years. They talked back to their officers, argued among themselves and frequently insisted on voting as to whether an order should be carried out or not. But their behavior following news of the White River massacre scarcely bears out Phelps' charges of cowardice. The handful of men, at least a third of whom were armed with weapons that couldn't be fired, set out immediately to bury the dead and rescue any who might have survived. Lieutenant Phelps remained on board the *Decatur* with the rest of her crew.

The dash for the blockhouse.

What the volunteers found was described in a letter written by Captain Hewitt:

"After two days hard work we reached the house of Mr. Cox (one of the settlers who had escaped to Seattle) which we found robbed. We next went to Mr. Jones, whose house had been burned to the ground; and Mr. Jones, being sick at the time, was burned in it. The body of Mrs. Jones was found some thirty yards from the house, shot through the lower part of the lungs, her face and jaws horribly broken and mutilated, apparently with the head of an ax. The bones of Mr. Jones were found, the flesh having been roasted and eaten off by hogs. Mr. Cooper, who had lived with Mr. Jones, was found about one hundred and fifty yards from the house, shot through the lungs. After burying the bodies we proceeded to the house of W. H. Brown*, a mile distant. Mrs. Brown and her infant, apparently ten months old, we found in a well, the mother stabbed in the back and head, and also in the lower part of the left breast, the child not dressed, but no marks of violence noticeable upon it. Mr. Brown was found in the house literally cut to pieces. We next went to the house of Mr. King, or the site of it, for it had been burned to the ground. Mr. Jones and the two children were burnt in the house, and the body of Mr. King, after being roasted, had been almost eaten up by hogs. Mrs. King was some thirty yards from the house. She had been shot through the heart and was horribly mutilated. Three children were saved, one the son of Mr. King and two of Mr. Jones".

When the volunteers returned to town on November 2 with their grizzly report no time was wasted in completing the Cherry Street blockhouse.

A few days later the Seattle volunteers were ordered back to the junction of the White and Green Rivers (near the present city of Auburn) to back up the forces of regulars from Fort Steilacoom commanded by Lieutenant W. A. Slaughter that was patrolling the river valleys for hostiles and guarding the trail from Naches Pass against the dreaded Klikitats of Eastern Washington.

The women of the village cooked a fine dinner for the volunteers the night before they left and presented them with a "handsome" flag. The next morning the little steamer *Traveler*, recently arrived on the Sound from San Francisco, put in at Yesler's wharf to transport the company, now fully armed with rifles from the *Decatur*, up the river. Soon after their departure an urgent message arrived at Seattle from Fort Steilacoom. Lieutenant Slaughter's company of regulars had been attacked by a large band of hostile Indians. One soldier had been killed, several wounded, and thirty head of horses and mules driven away. The Seattle volunteers were to dig in where they were. They wasted no time in beginning the now familiar task of cutting and trimming fir trees and building a log fort at the junction of the two rivers.

By the end of November, when Arthur Denny left for Olympia to serve as Speaker of the House in the Territorial Legislature, Seattle seemed as well protected as any settlement on the troubled Northwest frontier. The blockhouse stood firmly on the hill and the *Decatur* lay anchored close inshore. Most of the outlying settlers were now in Seattle and every man was armed. Lieutenant Slaughter's regulars and the volunteer company stood guard between the town and

---

*Captain Hewett was in error as to the name of this victim, which appears in the census list of that time as W. H. Brannon.

Naches Pass, which would soon be blocked with snow. The friendly local Indians were either in town or on Doc Maynard's reservation across the Sound where they weren't likely to be persuaded to join the enemy.

But any sense of security the settlers may have had was shattered on December 4 when a messenger arrived by canoe from the White River with the news that Lieutenant Slaughter had been killed by the Indians at the site of the original White River massacre.

Toward evening on December 3, word arrived at the volunteers' fort that Slaughter and his troops had arrived in the vicinity and camped for the night about four miles from the fort. Captain Hewitt, with a six-man guard under Corporal David Denny, set out at once to confer with him.

Slaughter and his company of about sixty regulars and volunteers from Captain William Wallace's Steilacoom detachment, badly mauled by the Indians, had marched all day in a drenching rain and were thoroughly soaked, chilled and exhausted. They had covered only eight miles through the fallen trees and dense underbrush of the unbroken forest. Contemporary accounts agree that Slaughter was urged to push on to the safety of the volunteers' fort but he had insisted that his men were too tired to make another move that night.

David Denny was, throughout his life, a man of action rather than of letters. He was content to help make history, not write it, and it is probably the lack of personal journals and memoirs that caused later historians to assign him a secondary role rather than the dominant one he deserves.

Fortunately his eye witness report of what happened at Lieutenant Slaughter's bivouac on the White River had survived:

"An Indian guide named Puyallup Tom accompanied Lieut. Slaughter through the Green River country where he was to meet with the company of volunteers of which I was a member. It was cold and raining nearly all day. When near the spot where they camped they saw an Indian dog skulking along in the underbrush. Puyallup Tom said that the dog's master was not far off and to "Closhe nanatch" (look out).

"Darkness came on before they reached the camp of the volunteers who were on the west side of the river. The Lieutenant found a small cabin in the opening in the woods and here he made camp for the night. They were all drenched to the skin so they stacked their arms and built large fires of fence rails around which the soldiers stood to dry. The Lieutenant did not put out any guards as he had not seen any Indians that day.

"He made his quarters in the cabin with his officers where they had a fire on the earth floor. As the night drew on the hooting of owls was heard. The guide told him it was the Indians signaling to each other but he said, 'No, you're mistaken'. Puyallup Tom begged that the fire be extinguished but the Lieut. refused.

"He sent a courier to the camp of the volunteers and three of their officers came to confer. The soldiers were around the bright fire and the Lieut. was sitting in the cabin when the Indians fired a volley into their midst killing Lieut. Slaughter instantly. The bullet came in between the logs striking him in the heart. He made no sound save the sharp intaking of his breath and fell over dead.

"Two of the soldiers were killed and several wounded. The men crowded into the little cabin and Puyallup Tom ran out and kicked the fires apart. The Indians withdrew for a time. Finally two men who were in a fence corner heard them creeping back and fired on them".

The Seattle volunteers, who Lieutenant Phelps of the *Decatur* insisted were a cowardly rabble, heard the gunfire and left the security of their fort for a night march through the black darkness of the forest to support the regulars. Along the way they met the troops from Fort Steilacoom retreating toward the fort carrying the body of their commander and the wounded in stretchers.

David Denny, who had been with Captain Hewitt at the scene of the ambush, later told how, when they took the body of the dead lieutenant from the cabin and began the retreat toward the volunteers' fort, they could hear the "victorious yells of the savages as they took posession of Slaughter's camp".

It had been impossible to carry the bodies of the other two dead soldiers as well as the wounded. When Corporal Denny led a burial detail back to the cabin the next morning they found the bodies robbed and scalped.

Soon afterward the Seattle volunteers were ordered to abandon their outlying fort and move closer to Seattle. Again they turned to with axes and saws to build still another blockhouse on Henry Van Asselt's farm on the Duwamish River about six miles south of Seattle. Patrols were sent out daily to scout the woods in all directions until January 25, when their three months term of enlistment expired and they returned to the village.

Meanwhile, the Navy as well as the Army had been having its troubles. Captain Sterrett of the *Decatur* had been removed from the active list by a court martial and replaced by Captain Guert Gansevoort on December 10. Captain Gansevoort's new command had, moreover, been reduced to the status of a derelict.

Three days before, while cruising off Bainbridge Island with Captain William Webster of the steamboat *Water Lily* as pilot, the sloop of war had sailed briskly onto an uncharted reef at the tip of the island. At low tide the crew stuffed her wounds with blankets and managed to get her across the Sound, where she was tied up to Yesler's wharf and, according to Lieutenant Phelps, *"the topmast and yards were sent on shore, hold broken out, battery removed to the wharf, and at high water hauled as far up on shore as it was possible to get her, so that when the tide was at the lowest ebb she was nearly 'high and dry'. An examination showed the keel, keelson, and side, up to the waterline, to be badly broken, the latter stove in, and the starboard side, from bridle-port to mainmast, and rail to keel, frame-knees, lining, and outside planking, excepting an inch of the outer surface, completely dry-rotted".*

While the crew of the *Decatur* worked day and night to make the old ship seaworthy again, the hostile Indians likewise hurried their preparations to wipe out Seattle and capture the *Decatur*'s guns and ammunition while she lay as helpless as a stranded whale on the mudflats. Although the Indians had won every battle with the regular and volunteer troops, they knew they were losing the war. They were short of food and arms; their women and children were starving in the swamps of the upper White River valley while the chiefs sought to negotiate "peace with honor". But the only person who could make peace was Governor Stevens and he was firmly on the record for hanging all the hostile Indians first and talking peace afterward.

In the face of Stevens' demand for unconditional surrender, Leschi and the other chiefs viewed an attack on Seattle as a last desperate gamble to secure the supplies and weapons they needed to keep fighting.

While the Indians gathered forces for the attack, the *Decatur*'s crew labored to restore her decayed hull and the volunteers patrolled the all-encompassing forest, the people of Seattle spent anxious days and nights waiting for the blow to fall. The nights were the worst in the candlelit cabins along the edge of the profound darkness of the forest. There were constant false alarms . . . as many as three in one night . . . when the candles were pinched out and everyone ran pell-mell for the blockhouse, which had been named Fort Decatur.

Even under such trying circumstances the pioneers didn't entirely lose their sense of humor. That Virginia gentleman, Hillory Butler, was a long time living down his role in one such midnight dash to the blockhouse. He and the Widow McConaha began the race for safety practically neck and neck, but the fleet-footed widow steadily outdistanced Butler, who kept shouting plaintively for her to "Wait for me!" But the widow kept on running.

Louisa Denny was especially delighted when the man who had ridiculed her husband's labors on the blockhouse came puffing into its shelter with his family, declaring himself to be an ardent exponent of preparedness.

On the night of January 18 the silence was shattered by a woman's scream and the loud explosion of a gun. The citizens made another dash for the blockhouse in their nightclothes. The marines who had been sleeping there and in Yesler's cookhouse grabbed their rifles and tumbled out to investigate.

The shot had been fired by fifteen-year-old Milton Holgate who was saving his sister from a sailor. The deserter from the *Decatur*, one John Drew, had attempted to crawl through the window of Miss Holgate's bedroom. She reacted swiftly, slamming the window down and pinning the deserter half in and half out of her room. Milton came running in response to her scream for help and shot the intruder through the head with a shotgun.

That night the crew of the *Decatur*, working by lantern light, finished the repairs to their ship. On the morning high tide she was moved to Yesler's wharf and her spars, guns and ammunition hoisted back on board. By evening she was at anchor, shipshape and in fighting trim again. Any chance the Indians might have had of capturing Seattle and the *Decatur* vanished during the night that Seaman Drew played his villianous and fatal role in the drama of the Battle of Seattle.

On January 25 the drama assumed comic opera overtones. First the Seattle volunteers, their three months term of service up, sauntered into town and disbanded. A little later the government survey steamer *Active* came into the bay and anchored near the *Decatur*. Governor Stevens was rowed ashore to make a speech to the citizens. Although he had consistently tended to exaggerate the perils of the Indian War and to demand fresh regiments of Army troops to defend the territory, he ridiculed the fears of the settlers, his address to them ending with the surprising assurance that *"there are not fifty hostile Indians in the territory, and I believe that the cities of New York and San Francisco will as soon be attacked by the Indians as the town of Seattle".**

The chief executive then went aboard the *Decatur* and tried to persuade Captain Gansevoort to abandon Seattle and accompany the *Active* on a cruise to Bellingham Bay. When the captain refused to be persuaded, Stevens departed in high dudgeon on the *Active*.

While the government steamer was still churning her way out of the bay, Indians began coming into town from the forest. They were peaceful Lake Indians under Chief Tecumseh, bringing their women and children with them and asking for protection, but friendly Indians moving out of the woods suggested unfriendly ones moving in.

Yarkekeman Jim had been dispatched by Captain Gansevoort to scout the forest between the village and Lake Washington and he confirmed the influx of hostiles with the report that a thousand Klikitats had crossed the mountains and that for two days the local Indians who had taken up arms . . . probably less than three hundred . . . had been ferrying them across the lake in canoes. The captain ordered his fighting division ashore to take up positions between the settlement and the forest. The *Decatur*'s brass howitzer was taken ashore in the ship's launch and set up behind the defensive line. A few marines under a sergeant were assigned to Fort Decatur, which had been armed with a pair of nine-pounders from the ship's battery.

The erstwhile Seattle volunteers were now in a somewhat embarrassing position. They had disbanded just as the war appeared to be beginning in earnest. A number of the ex-soldiers had spent their first hours as civilians refreshing themselves at the village bar and "bowling salloon" and refused to respond to appeals to either their patriotism or their fondness for their own scalps. Finally some thirty of the original eighty citizen soldiers agreed to return to service and were assigned to beef up the garrison at Fort Decatur and take over a sector of the defense perimeter.

Lieutenant Phelps claimed that during a late night tour of inspection it was discovered that "every soul of them had gone home to bed, leaving their guns behind to represent them".

According to accounts of some settlers, the *Decatur*'s fighting divisions were asleep in their hammocks in the blockhouse and cookhouse and only the citizen volunteers guarded the town that night. Louisa Denny felt that the discipline of most regulars and volunteers "left much to be desired". Many years later she told Victor Denny, Jr., *"David didn't trust anybody and slept with his rifle. Seattle was saved by a miracle and the Decatur's guns".*

This was only one of many areas in which the participants of the Battle of Seattle disagreed. A remarkable store of legend has grown up around that brief encounter. This much is certain, however:

Early in the morning of January 26 the shore parties were recalled to the *Decatur* for breakfast. As they left the line the hostile Indians began moving in closer to the town, a fact that was duly reported by the loyal Yarkekeman Jim. Henry Yesler carried the information to Captain Gansevoort, who ordered the long roll sounded. The marines and sailors left their breakfasts unfinished and returned to their posts.

---

*Pioneer historian Ezra Meeker, who was no admirer of the governor, had his own explanation for Stevens' sometimes bizarre actions. He insisted that in times of stress Stevens tended to drink more than was good for him.

The Indians had waited too long and missed the strategic moment to attack the town.

According to most contemporary sources, the final warning was sounded by Salmon Bay Curley's sister, a very fat squaw, who waddled along toward the beach at her best speed shouting, *"Hiu Klikitat copa Tom Pepper's house!"*, which meant in the Chinook jargon, a lot of Klikitats around Tom Pepper's house. Tom Pepper was an Indian who had a small dwelling on the eastern edge of the town.

It was then about eight o'clock in the morning and the January daylight was coming reluctantly to Seattle. Candles still burned in some of the cabins. Many of the men had just come in from the night watch and most of the townspeople were preparing or eating breakfast. The citizens of Seattle were the last to know that the attack on their town had actually begun. As they sat peacefully at their breakfast tables, Gansevoort ordered the howitzer to fire in the direction of Indian Tom Pepper's house. The *Decatur*'s main battery followed suit and a big shell screeched over the village rooftops, followed by a blood-curdling war cry from the forest and the crash of musketry from both sides.

Like the *Decatur*'s marines, the entire population of Seattle forgot all about breakfast and raced, with the precision of long practice, to the blockhouse. The unfortunate Hillory Butler again brought the rude humor of the frontiersmen down upon himself. Leaping from his bed at the sounds of battle, he was unable to find his pants and settled for his wife's red flannel petticoat, which he donned in great haste. This time, it was said, he passed the Widow McConaha and made a colorful entry to the blockhouse wearing the red flannel petticoat. Little Virginia Bell dived between the legs of a bemused marine who was watching Mr. Butler and brought the leatherneck down with a crash.

Mrs. Blaine, who had just had a baby, was carried to the blockhouse in a rocking chair. Louisa Denny, who was about to *have* a baby, took care of herself, little Emily Inez and their breakfast by herself and with amazing efficiency. David was on duty with the volunteers and she was alone with her child in the little house near the northern edge of the defended area, but throughout her life she was the archetype of the pioneer women and it took more than the roar of cannon, the crackle of small arms and the whooping of Indians to upset her presence of mind. She dumped the biscuits from the oven into her apron with one hand, grasped the little girl in her free arm and was on her way in a second.

Amid the confusion at the blockhouse David saw Louisa coming with her baby and her apron full of hot biscuits, along with the daughter of Moses Kirkland, one of the White River settlers who had escaped in time to avoid the massacre. As David ran out to help the young women, an excited volunteer inside the blockhouse fired off his rifle. Miss Kirkland fell beside Louisa and lay still. David carried her inside, apparently dead, but she had only fainted. The bullet had come so close that it cut off a lock of her thick black hair.

Little Emily Inez, not yet three years old, had no memories of any other aspect of the battle, but she wrote years later in *Blazing the Way*:

"A shot was accidently fired from a gun inside the fort, by which a pale-faced, dark haired lady narrowly escaped death. The bullet passed through a loop of her hair, below the ear, just beside the white neck. Her hair was dressed in an old fashioned way, parted in the middle on the forehead and smoothly brushed down over the ears, divided and twisted on each side and the two ropes of hair coiled together at the back of her head. Like a flashlight photograph, her face is imprinted on my memory; nothing before it or afterward for sometime can I claim to recall."

The Indians had emptied their rifles and muskets in the ragged volley in reply to the gunfire from the *Decatur*, and by the time they had reloaded the settlers were out of range and moving fast. All of them reached the blockhouse without being hit by either the Indians or the volunteers. As the Indians reloaded, young Milton Holgate, carrying the fowling piece with which he had defended his sister, ducked under the arm of Lieutenant Piexotto of the volunteers at the blockhouse doorway. He received an Indian bullet between the eyes and died instantly, the youngest and the first to fall in the Battle of Seattle. David Denny and the lieutenant carried him to a niche under the stairway where the body of Lieutenant Slaughter had lain after they brought him out from his defeat in the White River valley.

Fort Duwamish.

The only other recorded casualty occurred a little later when a young man named Robert Wilson stepped out on the second floor balcony of Mother Damnable's hotel for a better view of the fighting and had his neck broken by a bullet.

The gunfire from both sides continued briskly until early afternoon, when the Indians called a halt for lunch. While the braves had been firing on the town, the squaws had been busily butchering the citizens' cows and oxen and roasting the fattest over outdoor fires. The response to their call of "hyas muckamuck" (lots of food) was virtually unanimous and David Denny was relieved to observe the enemy's fire reduced to a few scattered shots. The lull gave him time to mend his trousers and his dignity. During the height of the battle he had bent over to open a keg of gunpowder and his pants had split from top to bottom. He retreated to a secluded corner and sewed up the split seam with very large stitches.

Captain Gansevoort also noted the much reduced volume of fire from the enemy and ordered his shore divisions to fall back to the boat landing at Yesler's wharf and return to the *Decatur* for *their* lunch. On their way they stopped at the blockhouse and took most of the women and children with them to the safety of the ship. Among the few who stayed were Louisa Denny and her small daughter. They felt safer with David than with the United States Navy.

The volunteers who remained at the blockhouse were hungry too, for few of them had finished breakfast. Some of the bolder ones made a foray on Carson Boren's cabin, which was not yet looted by the Indians, and returned with a good supply of flour, pork, sugar and potatoes. Private David Graham distinguished himself by baking a large batch of biscuits in a cabin within easy range of the Indian's barbeque grounds and returning with them, still piping hot, to the blockhouse.

After the luncheon lull the Battle of Seattle was never really renewed. Late in the afternoon the Indians fired a few face-saving vollies in the general direction of the town and the *Decatur* lobbed another round shot into the woods, but the attackers were running out of ammunition and enthusiasm.

Under cover of the early January darkness, the Indians plundered and burned most of the outlying homes in the village and retreated up the Duwamish, burning houses, barns and fences as they went.

The number of hostile Indians has been estimated as high as three thousand, including a thousand fierce Klikitats from Eastern Washington, but in fact the attack on Seattle was the last desperate gamble of the few hundred Puget Sound Indians who had chosen to take the path of war with Leschi of the Nisquallies.

The only outlying homes that were not burned were those of David and Louisa Denny and Thomas Mercer. These two families had always treated the Indians with particular kindness and, even in the heat of battle, the Indians had returned that kindness.

CHAPTER ELEVEN

Aftermath

The Battle of Seattle was ended, along with any lingering hopes of Leschi and the other war chiefs that they might prevail against the white men, but the citizens of Seattle didn't know it. They lived in fear of the new attack that Leschi had threatened. Every able bodied man set to work building a second blockhouse on top of a ridge just east of the Felker House on Jackson Street. The two forts and the entire central village were then enclosed in a stockade built of sawed lumber from Yesler's mill. This time there were no scoffers and the work of fully fortifying the town was accomplished in just a little over two weeks.

When the stockade was finished, families whose homes near the original blockhouse had not been burned returned to them during the day, but retreated to the security of the fort at night. Those from outside the village center remained in the blockhouse all winter.

In later years Louisa Denny recalled vividly that dreary, fear-ridden winter in the crowded log fort in what was left of Seattle.

There were no windows in Fort Decatur and seldom enough light for the women to sew or read. She told of one determined seamstress who taught herself to sew with her eyes closed to avoid the headaches brought on by trying to see what she was doing in the gloomy twilight of the fort.

During the short periods of grudging winter daylight, the women did manage to stitch together an American flag. After the siege was over, Louisa carefully preserved the flag until her death and was proud that "the red flannel of its stripes, although moth-eaten, is still red, the white cotton stars only a little yellowed, and the blue field not too badly faded".

It was said by the survivors of the Battle of Seattle that the stitches taken in the dim light of the fort weren't as fine as they might be, but "no Betsy Ross flag could be more precious".

The families crowded into the blockhouse had to take turns doing their cooking on the single stove, just as the founding party had had to do in the cramped cabin of the *Exact*. Water was carried up the hill from Yesler's mill by the men and older boys.

One of Louisa's most poignant memories was of the small children crying for milk, for most of the cows had been stolen or killed by the attacking Indians. Most Seattle families, like those of David and Louisa, had real affection for their household animals, bestowed pet names upon them and considered them almost members of the family. Three quarters of a century later Tom Mercer's daughter Susan told how she and her sister mourned the loss of their cow as one of the major tragedies of the battle.

It was in March, in the crowded upstairs family quarters of the blockhouse, now officially designated Fort Decatur, that a second daughter was born to David and Louisa. She was christened Madge Decatur Denny.

Although Leschi's little army was starving and almost out of ammunition and its remnants would soon retreat over the snowdrifts of Naches Pass to sanctuary in the Yakima country, rumors of attack continued throughout the winter of 1856. Mrs. Blaine wrote of one such report:

"A report which is believed by many has been brought recently that a formidable tribe from the British possessions have leagued with other hostile Indians and that 1200 of them are on their way here now. A steamer

started yesterday to look for them (as they will have to come by water) but I do not think she will find them as it is so easy to hide their canoes".

And so, as Mrs. Watt wrote, the citizens of Seattle *"lived in constant terror of an Indian attack, from the woods back of them, and from the water in front of them. It was a heartbreaking winter. Food was now giving out, and the children continued to cry for milk. On those days Arthur Denny wrote afterward, 'Those were times of pinching want and great privation such as we had never experienced except in the winter of '52-'53'.*

"Many of the settlers were leaving for Oregon and California as fast as they could get passage. It was hard for those who were left to see the others go. It took courage to remain. A few months after the battle there were but seventy-five or eighty men left, and less than a dozen families. It was Seattle's darkest hour.

"The Blaines accepted an offer from a church in Portland. Years later the pioneer minister and his wife returned to Seattle to spend the leisure years of their lives. 'The White Church' was closed. In these discouraging days the pioneers had nothing left to sustain them but their own integrity and faith".

In the spring the White River settlers returned to their claims to rebuild their homes and plant their crops, but they worked under the armed guard of a new company of volunteers commanded by Lieutenant Arthur Denny, and most of them continued to spend the nights at Fort Decatur. These farm crops were essential for survival. All trade and commerce was at a standstill in the Puget Sound country and each settlement was dependent upon its own resources.

It was not until late August that Captain Gansevoort was sure that Seattle was safe from Indian attack and ordered the sloop of war *Decatur* to set a course out of Elliott Bay for the last time. It was a sad farewell, for the ship and her crew had become old friends and she had become a symbol of security to the settlers.

Two more modern steam frigates, *Massachusetts* and *Active*, took station on Puget Sound to replace the *Decatur* and regular and volunteer forces were ringing the inland approaches to the Sound country with blockhouse forts, but the lurking fear remained. Long afterward Louisa Denny told her daughter Emily Inez that "for years afterward it was easy to imagine Indians everywhere".

The future of the village of Seattle, which had seemed so bright the previous summer, was in grave doubt in the aftermath of the ruinous Indian War. For a full decade afterward there was no new industry and few new settlers. All progress halted and there were times when even the most optimistic of the founders were in doubt as to whether the city they had platted could survive at all. The San Francisco building boom was ending and larger and more modern steam sawmills had been built elsewhere on the Sound. Yesler's mill kept running, but no longer on a 'round-the-clock basis. Elliott Bay was no longer a major port of call for coastal sailing ships in search of lumber cargoes.

Even stubborn Arthur Denny, who seldom recorded any doubts or fears, revealed in his later writings something of the despondency that beset the pioneers as they watched their high hopes blasted by long years of hard times and stagnation:

"Those who remained until the close of the war were so discouraged and so much in dread of another outbreak that they were unwilling to return to their homes in the country and undertake the task of rebuilding them. As a consequence it was years before we recovered lost ground to any extent. Business was generally stagnant. Little in the way of building or improvement was attempted. Roads that had been opened before the war had mostly become well nigh impassable and some of them entirely so. Active efforts were not resumed to improve the roads and open communications until 1866, a period of ten years".

It was during these dark days following the Indian War that Doc Maynard, once Seattle's most enthusiastic booster, lost all hope for his dream city and decided to become a farmer. In the summer of 1857 he traded the remaining 260 acres of his central Seattle claim to Charles Terry for his 320 acres at the now virtually abandoned site of New York Alki and moved across the bay to become, of all things, a farmer. Within a year or two Doc gave up his efforts to grow crops on the sandy soil of

The Denny's farmhouse in the swale.

Alki and sold out for $460, while Terry retained title to almost half the land within the town limits of Seattle.

David Denny was another who decided to return to the good earth and he was far better equipped to build a farm than was the amiable Maynard, who was becoming increasingly inclined to view his many disappointments through the distorted glass of a whiskey bottle.

David's decision was based on sound logic. Even had Seattle continued to grow and prosper, it would have been years before it expanded enough to make his isolated claim valuable as city property. The timber market was in a slump. Perhaps prosperity would return, but in the meantime his growing family had to eat. Farming, augmented by hunting and fishing, would insure that they did.

The original honeymoon cabin on the bay, although undamaged by the Indians, had no potential as a farmhouse. Despite the timber-cutting of the pre-war years, it was still hemmed in by the gigantic evergreen trees and jungle-like undergrowth of the forest. A lifetime of cutting and slashing would not have opened up this wilderness for farming.

He set out to build a new home on a relatively clear area of his claim, "the swale", at what later became Third Avenue and

Republican Street. The swale ran through the center of his claim, ending in a willow marsh bordering Lake Union. For years this was a favorite nesting place for wild ducks, which provided a major food item for the family table, but it was eventually drained and cleared to become a part of the Denny's Valley Farm which, according to their daughter Emily Inez, "grew apace until in after years it became the notable spot in all the district of what is now North Seattle".

Within three years ... by about 1860 ... David Denny had built a new log house and carved a productive farm from the wilderness. His skills as a hunter and fisherman had supplied meat for the table ... and he had even found the time and energy to build a small house of finished lumber at Second Avenue and Seneca Street near the village center. According to his eldest daughter, "It seems to have been Mr. Denny's plan to work out on his farm during the dry summer season and to reside down in the settlement in the winter".

This arrangement was surely a happy one for Louisa, who had had more than her share of isolation and loneliness in the depths of the forest.

In the years from 1857 to 1870 were probably the happiest ones in the lives of David and Louisa Denny and their children. By the time the new farm was cleared and productive and Louisa's new flower gardens were blooming, the fear of Indian attack had gradually faded. Unlike his brother Arthur, who viewed the new frontier with the coldly practical eye of a businessman intent on cashing in on its potential for profit, David loved the green and lovely land around him for himself ... the solitude of the beaches, the saltwater reaches of the inland sea with its leaping salmon and spouting whales, the deep forest with its wealth of game, and the distant challenge of the snow-capped mountains on the horizon.

Although he didn't share the political ambitions of his father and older brother, David Denny had gained the respect of his fellow citizens and would be called upon to serve in a variety of usually unpaid but responsible offices of local government. The pioneers of King County called him "Honest Dave". In this more cynical age such titles are sometimes given, with wry humor, to used car

Margaret Lenora Denny

dealers and real estate promoters of questionable ethics, but the less sophisticated frontiersmen in the nineteenth century meant exactly what they said. In a time and place when a man's word or handshake more often than not took the place of legal documents, David Denny's personal integrity was considered outstanding.

Those were good years for Louisa Denny, too. She shared her husband's love for the land and sea around them. She joined him on fishing expeditions and while he hunted in the forest she explored the mossy beds of wild flowers and the never ending variety of ferns and shrubs and wild berry patches. And, together, David and Louisa taught their children to share their love for the land around them.

Anna Louisa Denny.

There was no lack of children to be taught. The first to be born in the new farmhouse in the swale was another daughter, Abbie Lena, in the late summer of 1858. Then came the first son, John Bunyan, early in 1862, Anna Louise in 1864, and twin boys, David T. Denny II and Jonathan, on May 6, 1867. Jonathan lived only a few hours and was buried in the churchyard of the White Church near the graves of the two young men who had died in the Indian War. The youngest child, Victor Winfield Scott Denny, was born on August 9, 1869.

So slow was the growth of the settlement on Elliott Bay that even after little Victor was old enough to join the family expeditions into the woods, potentially dangerous wild animals were plentiful, only the wolves having retreated into the foothills of the Cascades to the east. Cougars were the most feared of the predatory animals, as Emily Inez Denny pointed out in *Blazing the Way:*

"It was springtime in an early year of pioneer times. *David and Louisa Denny were living in their log cabin in the swale, an opening in the midst of the great forest, about midway between Elliott Bay and Lake Union. Not very far away was their only neighbor, Thomas Mercer, with his family of several young daughters.*

"*On a pleasant morning, balmy with the presage of coming summer, as the two pioneers, David Denny and Thomas Mercer, wended their way to their task of cutting timber, they observed some of the cattle lying down in an open space, and heard the tinkling bell of one of the little band wandering about cropping fresh spring herbage in the edge of the woods. They looked with a feeling of affection at the faithful dumb creatures who were to aid in affording sustenance, as well as a sort of friendly companionship in the lonely wilds.*

"*After a long, sunny day spent in swinging the ax, whistling, singing and chatting, they returned to their cabins as the shadows were deepening in the mighty forest. In the first cabin there was considerable anxiety manifested by the mistress of the same, revealed in the conversation at the supper table:*

"'*David,' said she, 'there was something wrong with the cattle today; I heard a calf bawl as if something had caught it and 'Whiteface' came up all muddy and distressed looking'.*

"'*Is that so? Did you look to see what it was?'*

"'*I started to go but the baby cried so that I had to come back. A little while before that I thought I heard an Indian halloo and looked out of the door expecting to see him come down to the trail, but I did not see anything at all'.*

"'*What could it be? Well, it is so dark now in the woods that I can't see anything; I will have to wait until tomorrow'.*

"*Early the next morning, David went up to the place where he had seen the calves the day before, taking 'Towser', a large Newfoundland dog with him, also a long western rifle he had brought across the plains.*

"*Not so many rods from the cabin he found the remnants of a calf upon which some wild beast had feasted the day previous.*

"*There were large tracks all around easily followed, as the ground was soft with spring rains. Towser ran out into the thick timber hard after a wild creature, and David heard* something scratch and run up a tree and thought it must be a wild cat.

"He stepped up to a big fir log and walked along about fifty feet and looking up a giant cedar tree saw a huge cougar glaring down at him with great, savage yellow eyes, crouching motionless, except for the incessant twitching to and fro, of the tip of its tail, as a cat does when watching a mouse.

"Right before him in so convenient a place as to attract his attention, stood a large limb which had fallen and stuck into the ground alongside the log he was standing on, so he promptly rested his gun on it, but it sank into the soft earth from the weight of the gun and he quickly drew up, aiming at the chest of the cougar.

"The gun missed fire.

"He walked back along the log about twenty feet, took a pin out of his coat and picked out the tube, poured in fresh powder from his powder horn and put on a fresh cap, and this time he didn't miss.

"Hurrying back, David called for Mercer, a genial man always ready to lend a hand, to help him get the beast out to the cabin. The two men found it very heavy, all they could stagger under, even the short distance it had to be carried.

"As soon as the killing of the cougar was reported to the settlement, two miles away, everybody turned out to see the monster. Mrs. Catherine Blaine, the school teacher, who had gone home with the Mercer children, saw the animal and marveled at its size.

"Henry L. Yesler and all the mill hands repaired to the spot to view the dead monarch of the forest, none of whom had seen his like before. Large tracks had been seen in various places but were credited to timber wolves. This cougar's forearm measured the same as the leg of a large horse just above the knee joint. Such an animal, if it jumped down from a considerable height, would carry a man to the ground with such force as to stun him, when he could be clawed and chewed up to the creature's will.

"While the curious and admiring crowd were measuring and guessing at the weight of the cougar, Mr. Yesler called at the cabin. He kept looking about while he talked and finally said, 'You are quite high-toned here, I see your house is papered', at which all laugh-

Thomas Mercer

ed good-naturedly. Not all the cabins were 'papered', but this one was made quite neat by means of newspapers pasted on the walls, the finishing touch being a border of nothing more expensive than blue calico.

"At last they were all satisfied with their inspection of the first cougar and returned to the settlement."

Emily Inez, whose only recollection of the Battle of Seattle was the brief and shocking one of the apparent death of the young woman who ran with them toward the blockhouse, was old enough to recall vividly the family life and adventures on Valley Farm and at their winter home in the settlement. Her book thus provides an account of the growing-up years of David and Louisa Denny's children which is charming as well as authentic. It is evident in her writing that she shared her parents' deep and mystic love for the unspoiled wilderness in which she spent her childhood years:

"*The very thought of it*", she wrote, "*makes the blood tingle and the heart leap. No ele-*

Victor W.S. Denny

John B. Denny

ment was wanting for romance or adventure. Indians, bears, panthers, far journeys, in canoes or on horseback, fording rivers, camping and tramping, and all in a virgin wilderness so full of grandeur and loveliness that even very little children were impressed with the appearance thereof. The strangeness and newness of it all was hardly understood by the native white children as they had no means of comparing this region and mode of life with other countries and customs.

"Traditions did not trouble us; the Indians were generally friendly, the bears were only black ones and ran away from us as fast as their furry legs would carry them; the panthers did not care to eat us up, we felt assured, while there was plenty of venison to be had by stalking, and on a journey we rode safely, either on the pommel of father's saddle or behind mother's, clinging like small kittens or cockleburs.

"Familiarity with the coquettish canoe made us perfectly at home with it, and in later years when the tenderfoot arrived, we were convulsed with inextinguishable laughter at what seemed to us an unreasoning terror of a harmless craft.

"Ah! we lived close to dear nature then! Our play-grounds were the brown beaches or the hillsides covered with plumy young fir trees, the alder groves or the slashings where we hacked and chopped with our little hatchets in imitation of our elders or the Father of His Country and namesake of our state. Running on long logs, the prostrate trunks of trees several hundred feet long, and jumping from one to another was found to be an exhilarating pastime."

Busy as they were, and hard as their life might seem by the standards of today, David and Louisa found time to spend with their children, sharing skills as well as their old-fashioned moral precepts. The daughters as well as the sons of David Denny, the expert rifleman, were taught to handle firearms. As Emily Inez recalled:

"The boys learned to shoot and shoot well at an early age, first with shot guns, then rifles. Sometimes the girls proved dangerous with firearms in their hands. A sister of the writer learned to shoot off the head of a grouse at long range. A girl schoolmate, when scarcely grown, shot and killed a bear. My brothers and cousin, William R. Boren, were good shots at a tender age and killed numerous bears, deer, grouse, pheasants, ducks, wild pigeon, etc., in and about the district now occupied by the city of Seattle".

As each child grew old enough to join in family hikes and picnics, Louisa saw to it that the little boy or girl absorbed her love for the knowledge of nature ... the wild flowers, shrubs and birds with which the farm and its surroundings abounded. As Emily Inez recalled in *Blazing the Way:*

"The wild flowers and birds interested us deeply and every spring we joyfully noted the return of bluebirds and robins, the migrating wren and a number of other charming feathered friends. The high banks, not then demolished by grades, were smothered in greenery and hung with banners of bloom every succeeding season.

"We clambered up and down the steep places gathering armfuls of lillies (trillium), red currant (ribes sanguineum), Indian-arrow-wood (spiraea), snowy syringa (philadelphus) and blue forgetmenots and the yellow blossoms of the Oregon grape (berberis glumacea and aquifolium), which we munched with satisfaction for the soursweet, and the scarlet honeysuckle to bite off the honey-glands for the same purpose.

"The salmonberry and blackberry seasons were quite delightful. To plunge into the thick jungle, now traversed by Pike Street, Seattle, was a great treat. There blackberries attained Brobdignagian hugeness, rich and delicious".

Just as their mother overlooked the misery and discomfort of the landing at Alki in her delight at the profusion of new vegetation around her, her children came to view the rich cycle of growth and bloom around them as a part of the magic of growing up in an unspoiled frontier land. The memories of Emily Inez are rich with the fragrance of flowers that bloomed a century and more ago:

"In the garden the flowers bloomed often in December and January, as many as twenty-six varieties at once ... One New Year's day I walked down the garden path and plucked a fine, red rosebud to decorate the New Year's cake ... The pussy-willows began the floral procession of wildlings in January and the trilliums and currants were not far behind".

Louisa Denny was practical as well as sentimental when it came to plants and flowers. They needed tending as well as admiring, and she saw to it that the children did their share, as Emily Inez recorded:

"In the summertime we had work as well as play, out of doors. The garden surrounding our cottage in 1863, overflowed with fruits, vegetables and flowers. Nimble young fingers were made useful in helping to tend them. Weeding beds of spring onions and lettuce, sticking peas and beans, or hoeing potatoes, were considered excellent exercise for young muscles; no need of physical 'culchuah' in the school had dawned upon us, as periods of work and rest, study and play, followed each other in healthful succession.

"Having a surplus of good things, the children often went about the village with fresh vegetables and flowers, more often the latter, generous bouquets of fragrant and spicy roses and carnations, sweet peas and nasturtiums, to sell. Two little daughters in pretty, light print dresses and white hats were flower girls who were treated like little queens".

David and Louisa Denny were certainly dedicated to the pioneer American work ethic, but they were never too busy to share the beauties of their adopted frontier land with their children. When David drove the farm wagon into the forest to haul wood it was usually festooned with small children and there were usually numerous pauses along the way. They were, as Emily Inez recalled, *"begging to get off to gather flowers whenever they saw them peeping from their green bowers"*.

"Driving along through the great forest which stood an almost solid wall on either hand, we called 'O father, stop! stop; here is the lady-slipper place'.

" 'Well, be quick, I can't wait long'.

"Dropping down to the ground, we ran as fast as our feet could carry us to gather the lovely, fragrant orchid, Calypso Borealis, from its mossy bed. When the ferns were fully grown, eight or ten feet high, the little girls broke down as many as they could drag, and ran along the road, great ladies, with long green trains!"

This childhood memory of his daughter perhaps best gives insight to the character of David Denny; a character that made him unique among Seattle's founding fathers. While he shared the rigid moral code of his brother and was an ardent prohibitionist all his life, he was neither grim nor puritanical. Teetotaler though he was, he also had much in common with the amiable drunk, Doc Maynard . . . warmth, generosity, love of life and a profound sense of brotherhood with human beings of every race and creed.

The picture that comes down to us through the mists of time . . . of the young father pausing in his unending labors to let his small children pick wild flowers in the forest . . . may well be the most significant one.

The life of the children of the pioneers was a full and rich one, but it was not without its hazards. The family's brave little dog, Watch, always accompanied the children when they went into the forest or to the beach, and upon one occasion he kept a nine-foot cougar at bay in a hollow log while they beat a hasty retreat to safety.

During the unusually dry summer of 1868 the Denny children weren't able to walk to school because a forest fire raged between their farm home and the village, but according to Emily Inez, "We lost but little time on this account; it had not ceased before we ran past the tall firs and cedars flaming far above our heads".

Gale force winds are infrequent in the Puget Sound country, but when they come they wreak havoc with the huge evergreen trees with their shallow root systems. Walking down the same road on the way home from church on a windy day, Emily recalled, "When about half way home, a huge fir tree fell just behind us, and a half mile further on we turned down a branch road at the very moment that a tree fell across the main road usually traveled".

In her book, Emily Inez recalled two particularly violent windstorms:

"The first occurred when I was a small child. The wind had been blowing for some time, gradually increasing in the evening, and as night advanced becoming heavier every hour. Large stones were taken up from the high bank on the bay and piled on the roof with limbs broken from tough fir trees. Thousands of giant trees fell crashing and groaning to the ground, like a continuous cannonade; the noise was terrific and we feared for our lives. At midnight, not daring to leave the house, and yet fearing that it might be overthrown, we knelt and commended ourselves to Him who rules the storm.

"About one o'clock the storm abated and calmly and safely we lay down to sleep. The morning broke still and clear, but, many a proud monarch of the forest lay prone upon the ground".

Progress came so slowly to Seattle in the 1860's and 70's that even the youngest of the Denny children, Victor Winfield Scott, was able to experience the delights and dangers of a frontier huntsman's life. Like his brothers and sisters, he had been taught by his father to handle a gun soon after he learned to walk. He could speak the Indian dialects fluently, hunted and fished with the Indian boys and loved to don a blanket to imitate an Indian, jumping fences and uttering disconcertingly authentic war whoops.

One late November afternoon Victor and his brother David, who was two years his elder, took a shotgun and hiked along the trail to Lake Union where they borrowed a small fishing canoe from old Tsetseguis, an Indian who lived at the landing. They then paddled out to look at some muskrat traps they had set. The subsequent events were described by their older sister in her book:

"It was growing quite dark when they thought of returning. For some reason they decided to change places in the canoe, a very 'ticklish' thing to do. When one attempted to pass the other, over went the little cockle-

shell and both were struggling in the water. The elder managed to thrust one arm through the hunting bag worn by the younger and grasped him by the hair, said hair being a luxuriant mass of long, golden brown curls.* Able to swim a little he kept them afloat although he could not keep the younger one's head above water. His cries for help reached the ears of a young man, Charles Nollop, who was preparing to cook a beefsteak for his supper . . . he threw the frying pan one way while the steak went the other, and rushed coatless and hatless to the rescue, with another man, Joe Raber, in a boat.

"An older brother of the two lads, John B. Denny, was just emerging from the north door of the big barn with two pails of milk; hearing, as he thought, the words 'I'm drowning,' rather faintly from the lake, he dropped the pails unceremoniously and ran down to the shore swiftly, found only an old shovel-nosed canoe and no paddle, seized a picket and paddled across the little bay to where the water appeared agitated; there he found the two boys struggling in the water, or rather one of them. The other was already unconscious. Arriving at the same time in their boat Charley Nollop and Joe Raber helped to pull them out of the water. The long curls of the younger were entangled in the crossed cords of the shot pouch and powder flask worn by the older one, who was about to sink for the last time, as he was exhausted and had to let go of the younger, who was submerged.

"Their mother reached the shore as the unconscious one was stretched upon the ground and raised his arms and felt for the heart which was beating feebly.

"The swimmer walked up the hill to the house; the younger, still unconscious, was carried, face downward, into a room where a large fire was burning in an open fireplace, and laid down before it on a rug. Restoratives were quickly applied and upon a partial recovery he was warmly tucked in bed. A few feverish days followed, yet both escaped without serious injury.

"Mrs. Tsteseguis was much grieved and repeated over and over, 'I told the Oleman not to lend that little canoe to the boys and he said, 'O it's all right, they know how to manage a canoe'.

"Tsetseguis was also much distressed and showed genuine sympathy, following the rescued into the house to see if they were really safe".

Such near disasters were rare among the self-reliant children of David and Louisa Denny, and most of their memories were good ones.

In 1859 old John Denny, having heard that Seattle was doomed to become a ghost town, stubbornly sold his prosperous Oregon farm and moved to his sons' struggling village on Puget Sound, providing it with a much loved elder statesman and the Denny children with that essential to a well rounded childhood, grandparents. Emily Inez recalled that on their wagon rides into the forest with their father, "We found the way to the opening in the woods, where in the midst thereof, grandfather sat making cedar shingles with a drawing knife. Huge trees lay on the ground, piles of bolts had been cut and the heap of fragrant shingles, clear and straight of the very best quality, grew apace".

It was only natural that Louisa, who had brought Christmas across the plains to Smaquamox, should provide her children with Seattle's first Christmas tree at the little winter home "down town" . . . "a handsome Douglas fir, reaching from floor to ceiling, loaded with gay presents and blazing with tapers".

Afterward a much larger community Christmas tree was set up outside Yesler's cookhouse, with gifts for all the children of the settlement, a tradition that continued until Seattle grew from a village to a town.

For many years after 1867, David Denny found time to keep a brief daily journal. His notations dealt almost exclusively with the day-to-day routine of himself and his family. There is no record of such major events as the incorporation of Seattle as a city, its rejection by the Northern Pacific as the western terminus of the transcontinental railway, or Washington Territory's achievement of statehood. The sparsely worded entries in the little notebooks do, however, give considerable insight on pioneer life in general and the life and times of David Denny in particular.

---

*The author may have engaged in a bit of literary license here. According to family lore, Victor did have "golden curls" as a very small child, but by the time he had grown old enough to go hunting and fishing with his brother his hair had turned as black as an Indian's.

The Territorial University shortly after its construction.

On January 1, 1867, with the family spending the winter at their little house in town, he *"spent half day about business and then went to place (the farm in the swale) and boarded up west end of calf shed"*. The next day he *"set fire to log and peeled bark; worked on road"* (from the log farmhouse to the shore of Lake Union) and *"made a staff for compass"*.

On January 3 he used the new staff and his surveying compass to *"survey the line between me and Pontius"*. The next day he *"went to Lake Union and measured distance from my corner to ¼ post"*. On January 6, which was a Sunday, he *"heard Whitworth preach"*. Over the years the Sunday entries were the same; he either went to hear a frontier minister preach or *"stayed home and read"*.

Already an indefatigable prospector, he frequently took time from his hunting, woodcutting and surveying to look for indications of mineral resources in the area. On January 7

The Denny house overlooking Lake Union.

he "*went to lake place to look at building site*" (where he was planning to build a bigger house) and "*prospected for coal and found ledge of sandstone*". The next day he "*hunted. got one pheasant. Found rusty water north of University*". He did find a small coal deposit on his claim, which he later worked commercially for a time, but the rusty water on the hill behind the town didn't lead to the discovery of iron ore.

On January 14 he "*hauled load of bark for White, got venison of Lewis*" and "*visited Terry*". The latter entry referred to Charles Terry, the erstwhile boon companion of the miners aboard the *Exact* and proprietor of New York Alki, who was dying of tuberculosis. Thereafter, following his long days' work, he spent many nights at the bedside of his fellow pioneer. On February 15 he "*sat up with Terry*" for the last time and, on the 17th, "*wrote Terry's obituary*". Charles Terry, on his deathbed, begged "Honest Dave" to accept the guardianship of his children, a trust that he accepted and performed faithfully for many years.

In another February entry he recorded, "*Snowed in squalls all day. Swept out church and trimmed lamps*". He also attended a meeting of the Board of Regents of the Territorial University, of which he was a member and, when the school custodian got sick Regent Denny took over the humble duty of tolling the bell to summon the students to class. One morning the great iron clapper broke loose from the bell, high in the tower above his head, missed him by inches and embedded itself in the wooden floor beside him.

In the early spring he *"hunted bear". with the little fox terrior Watch.*

"Hauled hay home. Got 'George' shod" (all the horses and other domestic animals of David and Louisa Denny had pet names); *"Finished road to landing at Lake Union; cut and welded a wagon tire; invented and built a 'comb' so children can harvest berries without getting scratched; mended shoes for Louisa and children"* and *"went to singing school"*.

His daughter Emily noted that her father *"had a fine ringing tenor voice and could carry a tune very well. It was a treat to hear him as he sawed or chopped in the great forest singing verse after verse of the grand old hymns"*.

On May 6 he recorded, *"Twins born, one at 10 minutes past 11; one at 20 minutes to 12 o-clock M. Younger died at 7 p.m."*.

In the fourteen years between the Indian attack of 1856 and 1870, the family of David and Louisa Denny had grown a good deal faster than had the town of Seattle. Olympia was still the biggest settlement on Puget Sound, with a population of about 1,500, but David Denny didn't share the anguish of the other town fathers over the failure of their community to quickly become the metropolis of the Pacific Northwest.

He hadn't crossed the plains and mountains to sell town lots and get rich. His objective had been a comfortable home for Louisa and himself and, he hoped, a large and healthy family of children.

And by 1870 he had achieved his objective.

John B. Denny and first wife

CHAPTER TWELVE

The Later Years

Although Seattle's growth had been less than spectacular in the nearly twenty years since the landing of the Denny party at Alki Point . . . the population increase had averaged only about fifty a year . . . the seeds of expansion had been planted.

In 1861, as Speaker of the House in the Territorial Legislature, Arthur Denny had joined forces with Seattle's new Methodist minister, the Reverend Daniel Bagley, to reshuffle the location of the territory's major institutions. A bill was quickly passed moving the capital from Olympia to Vancouver and the penitentiary from Vancouver to Port Townsend. In return, the territorial university was assigned to Seattle and Reverend Bagley was named chairman of the board of university commissioners (with the cooperation of father John Denny, who happened to be Chairman of the Education Committee of the Territorial Legislature that session).

The Territorial Supreme Court subsequently ruled that the capital move was illegal, Vancouver lost the penitentiary and so did Port Townsend but, to the amazement of everybody, especially the Legislature, Seattle got the university.

Although the federal government had set aside valuable timber lands to finance such an institution of higher learning, it merely *reserved* them and did not actually authorize their sale without Congressional approval.

Chairman Bagley, on cooperation with Abe Lincoln's newly appointed Territorial Registrar of Public Lands . . . Arthur Denny . . . went ahead and sold 20,000 acres of the public land anyway, raising $30,000 to build the university. That was a lot of money in those troubled times. When disbursed among the town's merchants, artisans and laborers, as it soon was, it represented more than $1,300 per family, which was more cash money than most of them had seen in the last ten years.

It was at this point that Arthur Denny made his only known gift of land . . . eight and a third acres on a steep cliff separated from the populated area by a half mile of almost impenetrable forest. Terry and Lander were prevailed upon to donate the additional land needed to meet the legislature's requirement for a ten-acre campus. Astute business man that he was, Arthur was doubtless aware that his gift was more in the nature of an investment. The community would have to build streets to the university site, which would greatly increase the value of his remaining 310-odd acres, there was that $30,000 windfall to be divided up and, after all, the land hadn't cost him anything in the first place.

On May 20, 1861, the cornerstone of the main university building was laid and before the year was out it stood on the newly cleared hill above the town as the grandest building in the territory. There was considerable outrage at Olympia and in Washington, D.C., especially when it was found that there was only one citizen of Washington Territory qualified to enroll in college level courses, but John Denny and the Reverend Bagley journeyed to the national capital to smooth things out. They were assisted greatly by Arthur Denny, who had recently been elected Delegate to Congress, and by President Lincoln, who remembered fondly his leap with John Denny from the upper floor of the Illinois statehouse.

Congress passed measures retroactively legalizing the Reverend Bagley's entirely illegal sale of public lands for the construction of the University of Washington.

For a long time the university operated as a grammar school . . . Emily Inez Denny was a student there at the age of twelve . . . but its initial construction had gone a long way toward ending the long post-Indian War depression at Seattle.

By 1869 the community had recovered sufficiently to be accorded the dignity of legislative incorporation as a town. David Denny, whose farming and logging operations were prospering, was chosen as one of the first town trustees. When a school district was organized soon afterward, he was elected a member of the first school board.

Two years later his affairs were going so well that he was able to have the long-planned new home built for Louisa and the children . . . one that was far different from the one-room log cabin where they had begun their married life eighteen years earlier. The fourteen-room house of simple Colonial style without the carpenter Gothic towers and gingerbread trim that was coming into vogue at that time, was located on the homestead farm, but further east than the old home and overlooking Lake Union rather than the bay. Within a few years it was surrounded by another of Louisa's flower gardens and an orchard and, according to the Seattle *Times*, "was, after its completion, one of the most commodious and important houses in the city".

In 1873 Seattle received a blow almost as calamitous as the Indian War. The long-awaited Northern Pacific Railroad had begun construction of its "Pacific Division" from the village of Kalama on the Columbia River to tidewater on Puget Sound. Both Seattle and Olympia, the region's two largest towns, confidently expected to receive the railroad terminus. Instead the Northern Pacific chose to locate it on Commencement Bay and promote its own new town to be called Tacoma.

Again the more timid individuals and businesses moved away, many of them to Tacoma. By this time, however, there were alternative means of transportation available. Roads had been cut and graded through the tidewater forests to connect the principle settlements, and a fleet of little steamboats plied the waters of Puget Sound, carrying freight, passengers and mail. Seattle survived and even continued to grow despite the efforts of the railroad to throttle it. The census of 1880 showed that, with a population of 3,533, Seattle was clearly the metropolis of Washington Territory. Olympia was a distant second with 1,532, and the Northern Pacific's town of Tacoma a disappointing third with only 1,098.

Few of the original "founding fathers" who had landed from the *Exact* three decades earlier were still in Seattle to celebrate this modest triumph. Charles and Lee Terry had both died in the late 1860's, Lee in New York and Charles in Seattle, but both of tuberculosis. John Low continued to live placidly on his dairy farm near Olympia, and William Bell was among those who had left for more peaceful regions after the Indian War. He returned many years later, but neither he nor Carson Boren contributed much to the later development of the city.

Doc Maynard had died in 1873 and his funeral was the largest Seattle had seen to that time, held in Yesler's Pavillion, a big wooden building that had replaced the cookhouse as the town's meeting place. One of his last acts had been the gift of a plot of land east of town for a Masonic cemetery, and he was the first to be buried in it. Two years later, in 1875, even more people turned out to pay their last respects to patriarchal John Denny, dead at the age of 82. He was buried on David's claim north of town. The five-acre tract had been given to the town by David and Louisa as its first park, but Seattle was closely surrounded by one giant park and it was believed more practical to use it, at least for the time being, as burial ground.

The cemetery was moved in later years and Denny Park became an oasis of green at the busy corner of Dexter and Denny Avenues in the downtown Seattle commercial area, although in later years part of the park area was, despite the strong objections of the descendants of David and Louisa, used by the city to construct an office building and parking lot for the municipal park department.

During these years David and Louisa gave other plots of land from their claim, for

Old Denny School.

Cupalo from Denny School in Denny Park.

churches, schools and charitable institutions and not for any expected gain. The Seattle Children's Home is still located on land given originally by them.

The hospitable home overlooking the lake became a mecca for itinerant preachers, new arrivals seeking advice on business and land purchase matters from "Honest Dave", and travelers who were down on their luck and seeking a handout. No one was ever turned away. For a good many years young William Boren was an eighth child in the family. The marriage of his parents had broken up and his father, Carson, was frequently gone for long periods of time, searching the length of the Pacific Coast for gold or new hunting grounds or peace of mind. Along with the other children, David taught William Boren the precepts of Christianity and temperance along with the skills of the woodsman and hunter.

As roads and scattered homes thrust further north, the family camping and hunting expeditions frequently extended to the wilderness area beyond Green Lake, at a mineral springs the Indians called Licton. And when time permitted, David explored the western slopes of the Cascade Mountains, prospecting for gold and silver. As Seattle grew and progress pressed in upon him, the solitude of the high country became increasingly a refuge to him.

And Seattle did grow . . . at an astounding rate. Between 1880 and 1889 the population increased four hundred percent, from 5,000 to over 20,000.

Then, in the summer of 1889, another apparent disaster struck. Fire broke out in a downtown cabinet shop and quickly spread through the business district. There had been a long dry spell and pressure in the water mains was low. The best efforts of the volunteer fire companies and engines from other towns sent in to help were unavailing. By nightfall, sixty square blocks had been reduced to glowing ashes . . . all the docks along the downtown waterfront and virtually the entire business and commercial area of the town.

The Great Fire proved to be something of a disguised blessing, however. The Seattle of 1889 had been a tinder town of wooden buildings and planked streets. Within a year it was rebuilt with stone and masonry business blocks and paved streets. And in the process, to everyone's surprise, it had doubled its population again . . . to more than 40,000, or eleven times the official figures of the last federal census.

The city had finally spread north to David Denny's once isolated claim and he had formed the real estate firm of D.T. Denny & Son in partnership with 28-year-old John B. for the purpose of selling city lots. The enterprise was highly successful, and new homes sprang up

THE GREAT SEATTLE FIRE—1889

along streets that Louisa and David had named for their religious and temporal convictions . . . Prohibition, Temperance and Republican, among others.

Arthur Denny, whose original claim encompassed a major portion of the city center, was content to let the Seattle boom remunerate him handsomely for his original investment of "muscle and timber". The general store, which he had founded without personal investment, had expanded into the prosperous mercantile establishment of Horton, Denny and Phillips, and thence to the town's principle banking establishment, Dexter Horton & Company, with Arthur Denny as vice president. Arthur was of a naturally conservative and cautious nature and being a banker made him more so. Others could risk their money building electrical generating plants, water systems, street railways and the other amenities needed to keep a growing city growing even faster. He would stick to well secured mortgages and the natural accretion of wealth through his downtown land holdings.

David acted on a very different principle. As fast as his land made money for him he plowed it into ventures that would create new jobs, new homes and new population growth for Seattle. On Lake Union, at what had been the eastern edge of his claim, he built the Western Mill, the biggest sawmill in King County. Then he organized the Union Water Company to lay mains under the new streets of his subdivisions, which had been cleared and graded by his Washington Improvement Company.

After pausing long enough to build Louisa a grand new mansion on Temperance Street, (now Queen Anne Avenue), he launched himself into riskier and more expensive civic projects . . . the building of electric railways.

The first successful street car line using electric power had gone into operation only two years earlier, in 1888, at Richmond, Virginia, and the electric trolley was still generally considered to be a dangerous and newfangled contraption. Seattle had had a few miles of street railway line served by horse-drawn cars since early in 1886. The northern terminus of the line was near the new Denny mansion on Temperance Street.

The horse cars were replaced by electric trolleys early in 1889 and it quickly became apparent to David Denny that this marvelous new means of rapid transit was an ideal means of opening up unimproved land

David and Louisa Denny's mansion on Temperance Street, Queen Anne Hill.

to residential development. The theory made a good deal of sense; extend a car line into the hinterland, making it possible to get to work or downtown for shopping quickly and economically, and they would buy lots and build houses along that car line.

It was, in a sense, a modern form of pioneering, which may have been one reason David Denny took to it with such enthusiasm. No doubt the fact that his second son, David T. Denny II, had become an electrical engineer and strong advocate of the electric trolley also had its effect.

In any event, the two David Dennys, father and son, in 1890 embarked upon the most ambitious . . . and disastrous . . . street railway building venture in the city's history.

The Rainier Power & Railway Company line was built in three sections under three separate city ordinances. The first of these, authorized in June of 1890, ran from East Lynn Street, then the north city limits, down

Early electric trolley on Rainier Power & Railway line.

the east shore of Lake Union to a rural lane marked Filbert Street on the plat of North Seattle. The second section, authorized early in 1892, began downtown at Third and Yesler and continued, according to its franchise, "along 3rd St., 4th St., Union, 8th Ave., Pike St., 9th Ave., Stewart St., 15th Ave., Denny Way, Pontius Ave., Roy St. and Harvard Ave. N.", connecting at Valley Street with the section of line built earlier.

The third section was built under a King County franchise granted in August, 1891, and ran from the East Lynn Street terminus of the first section through Ravenna Park, across an old lift bridge at the present site of the University Bridge, and on north through increasingly uninhabited wilderness to what is now 45th Avenue Northeast. Beyond that point there was nothing but forest and meadow, but it continued north for a mile into the unplatted wilderness, looped in a southeasterly direction and terminated in the middle of nowhere in the vicinity of 22nd Avenue Northeast.

This street car line to nowhere consistently lost money from the time its first section was placed in operation, but David Denny was not a man to give up easily. Instead of retrenching, he expanded.

On August 3, 1893, David Denny & Son bought out the pioneer street railway of L.H. Griffith, the Seattle Electric Railway and Power Company, which accounted for about half the 70 miles of electric and cable lines then operating in and around Seattle.

The newly acquired line served the more profitable heavily populated sections of the city, and given reasonably stable economic conditions the consolidated system would probably have survived. After all, David Denny had become one of the richest men in town, most contemporary sources placing the value of his estate in the neighborhood of three million dollars . . . a tremendous fortune in that time and place.

Unfortunately, much of his wealth was in still undeveloped land . . . land that he had hoped his trolley lines *would* develop. His property taxes were based on speculative values and ran to thousands of dollars a year. Many thousands of dollars more were in accounts receivable and many purchasers never bothered to pay him for the land upon which they built, or the lumber for their houses.

"Old man Denny's got plenty", they rationalized. "He don't need it". They were also no doubt aware that, unlike his older brother and such other wealthy pioneers as Henry Yesler and Dexter Horton, he was reluctant to sue his neighbors.

But it was the long-remembered Panic of 1893 that wiped out the fruits of more than four decades of privation, danger and toil. The ink was hardly dry on the transfer of title when both of his lines were swept into bankruptcy. Everything else he owned was soon swept into the financial whirlpool that rose around him.

Over the years his fellow citizens had chosen him to represent them in positions of trust . . . town trustee, school board member, city councilman, university trustee and probate judge. When his many business enterprises employed hundreds of men, he paid them more than the prevailing wages and, although it was general knowledge that he had been frequently robbed by dishonest employees, he had never prosecuted one.

According to his daughter, *"When urged to close down his mill, as it was running behind, he said, 'I can't do it; it would throw a hundred men out of employment and their families will suffer.' So he borrowed money, paying a ruinous rate of interest, and kept on, hoping that business would improve; it did not and the mill finally went under. A good many employees who received the highest wages for the shortest hours, struck for more, and others were full of rage when the end*

David Denny on front platform of first trolley to the University District; his son David, Jr. on the rear platform.

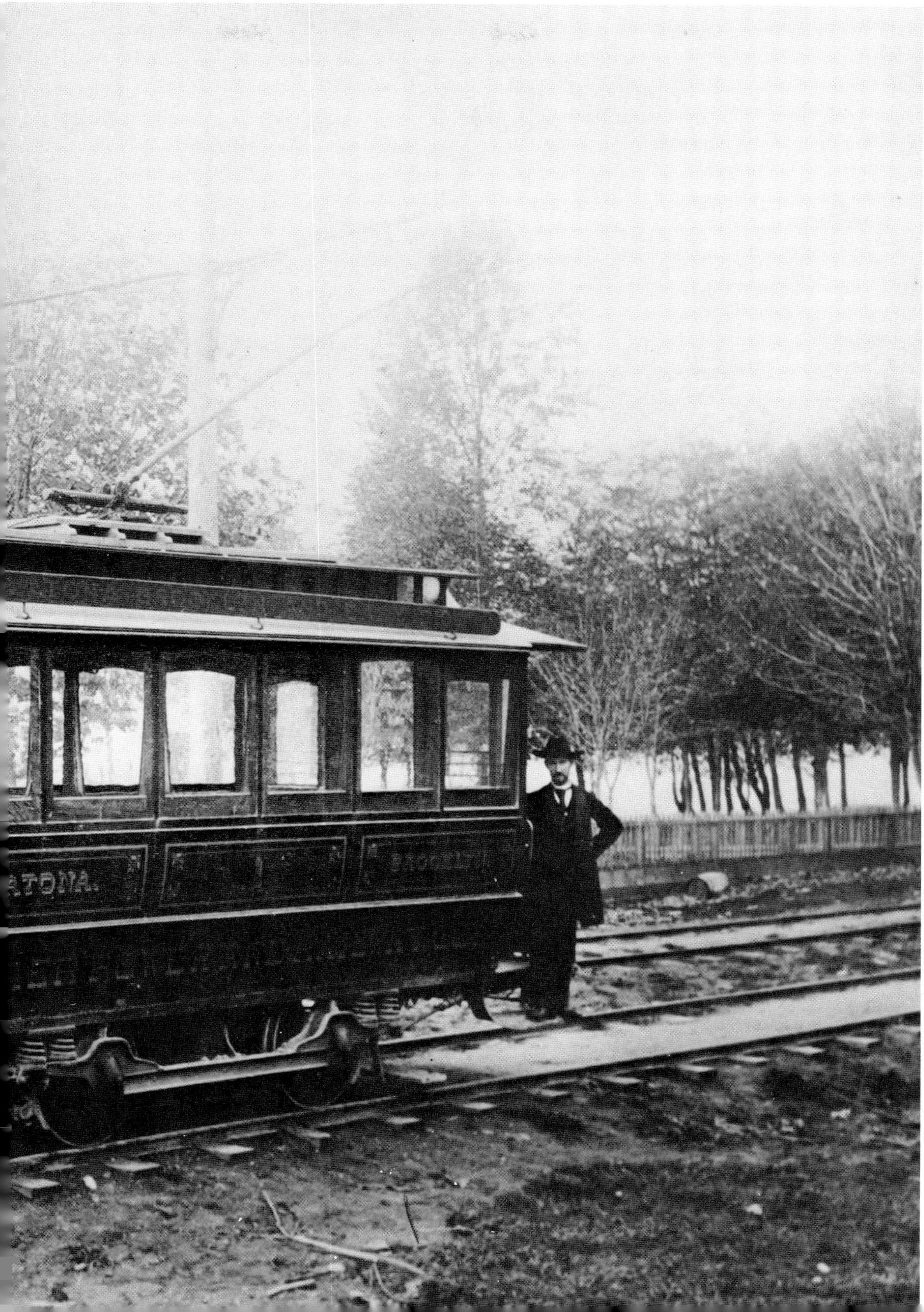
ATONA.

David Denny, second from left, front row, as member of Seattle City Coun-cil.

came and there were only a few dollars due on their wages".

All this was forgotten when the crash came. The city treasurer at that time was an amiable ex-baker named Adolf Krug. The city was operating on credit in the form of treasurer's warrants, which couldn't be cashed, but paid liberal interest to their holders. The more conservative members of the business community who had held onto their dollars were willing to buy city warrants at a discount as fast as Krug could stamp them "un-

The anti-Chinese riots.

paid for lack of funds". On the other hand, there were numerous substantial citizens who were in financial trouble and needed cash loans, and the ingenious Krug hit upon a plan to satisfy both groups. When the treasury took in a sack of cash he lent to his needy friends, permitting him to issue more warrants to be sold to his prosperous friends.

In a final effort to stave off disaster, David Denny applied to the treasurer for a loan. Most of those who borrowed city funds from Krug had simply given him personal IOU's, but David insisted upon securing his loan with a properly executed mortgage on real estate appraised at more than three times its amount.

When the financial chaos in the city treasury was discovered, Krug was arrested and a major scandal ensued, providing a field day for those who bore grudges against the man who was reputed to have been "the richest man in town".

Much of the ill feeling against David Denny and other civic leaders had festered for seven years, since they had strongly opposed the actions of a mob intent on driving the Chinese out of Seattle. The Chinese laborers had been imported to build the transcontinental railways, but when the work was completed they were viewed as a threat by the white and Indian labor force of the Pacific Northwest because they were willing to work harder and longer for less money. Emily Inez Denny recorded some of her memories of the bitterness of the mob against her father, who was particularly well known for his lack of racial prejudice:

"Previous to and during the anti-Chinese riot in Seattle, which occurred on Sunday, February 7th, 1886, he received a considerable amount of offensive attention. In the dark district of Seattle, there gathered one day a forerunner of the greater mob which created so much disturbance, howling that they would burn him out. 'We'll burn his barn,' they yelled, their provocation being that he employed Chinese house servants and rented ground to Mongolian gardeners. The writer remembers that it was a fine garden, in an excellent state of cultivation. No doubt many of the agitators themselves had partaken of the products thereof many times, it

being one of the chief sources of supply of the city.

"The threats were so loud and bitter against the friends of the Chinese that it was felt necessary to post a guard at his residence. The eldest son was in Oregon, attending the law school of the University; the next one, D. Thos. Denny, Jr., not yet of age, served in the militia during the riot; the third and youngest (Victor W.S. Denny, also a crack shot); remained at home ready to help defend the same. The outlook was dark, but after some serious remarks concerning the condition of things, Mr. Denny went upstairs and brought down his Winchester rifle, stood it in a near corner and calmly resumed his reading. As he had dealt with savages before, he stood his ground. At a notorious trial of white men for unprovoked murder of Chinese, it was brought out that 'Mr. David Denny, he fliend (friend) of Chinese and Injun.' "

The Denny's Chinese cook, the focus of the mob's indignation, was also a formidable adversary, carrying a long-barreled frontier colt strapped to his arm under his voluminous sleeve. The mob got as far as Licton Springs, but had second thoughts and withdrew.

The bitterness of the Chinese riots lingered for a long time. The bigots, who were in the majority, were able to take revenge at the polls upon those of the law and order faction who had political ambitions. Arthur Denny was defeated for reelection as mayor by a politically unknown late-comer. Judge Thomas Burke, one of the most widely respected men in the territory, was defeated in a try for the United States Senate more than two decades afterward on the strength of that carefully preserved hatred.

Since David Denny had no ambitions for high political office, the haters had to bide their time until the Krug affair gave them their opportunity. No distinction was made between those who had obtained unsecured loans from the city treasury and the few like him who had pledged more than ample collateral. The man who had done more than any other to build Seattle was loudly charged with being one of those who had "robbed the city".

The strident attacks on his lifelong reputation for complete honesty were a worse blow to David Denny than the loss of his fortune and seemed the culmination of the series of tragedies which had beset him and his family in the later years. As a lifelong worker in the Methodist Church, he had been sent in 1888 as a delegate to the General Conference of the church at New York. Louisa and the children went with him on his first eastward crossing of the continent, by the Canadian Pacific Railway to Montreal and New York. Of that ill-starred journey and its aftermath the eldest daughter wrote:

"In the latter place (New York) they met their first great sorrow, in the death, after a brief illness, of the beloved youngest daughter (Anna Louisa, then 24 years of age), the return and her burial in her native land by the sundown seas. Soon followed other days of sadness and trial; in less than a year the second daughter, born in Fort Decatur, passed away, and others of the family hovered on the brink of the grave, but happily were restored".

The eldest son, John Bunyon Denny, then 27 years of age, was stricken by the unnamed malady, as was the youngest, Victor Winfield Scott, whose family nickname was "Win". Although weak and ailing, John recorded in his journal the events of that tragic January of 1889:

"Jan. 1: Madge no better . . . very sick . . . Win very weak but somewhat improved. 13th day of my illness. Sat up about 20 minutes. Hope and pray that Madge and Winnie may get well".

"Jan. 2: Doctor reports Made and Win somewhat improved. Sat up in a chair a good part of the day. Carrie (his wife) *not very well. Made and Win improved".*

There followed several entries that indicated that both Madge and young Victor were getting better, but on January 15 he wrote: *"Madge too sick to see me"* and, the next day, *"Madge delerious and worse. Win better".*

---

[1] Four years later David Denny attended another conference in New York, traveling via the new transcontinental railway that he and Dr. Smith had agreed would some day establish its western terminus at Smiths Cove. Its line skirted American Falls, where the Denny wagon train was attacked by Indians four decades earlier. Of this experience he wrote in later years:

"In 1892 I went East over the Great Northern. I was thinking of my first experience (with the hostile Indians) in Montana when I reached that state, when all of a sudden we rounded a curve and passed below the falls. I knew them in a minute, and instantly those old scenes and trying times came back to me in a way that was altogether too realistic for comfort".

And finally, on January 17, "*Wild storm, some rain. Madge died at 3 a.m. Died peacefully trusting in Jesus*". The following day John "*went to see the last of my sister Madge on earth. She seemed to be at rest. Dear sisster. Arthur and W.B. Denny were at the house.* On January 18 John's journal ended with the notation: "*Madge's funeral was held at home at 11 a.m. Laid at rest beside our sister Annie. God is with us still. Win looks better*".

On the day of Madge's death, David wrote: "*This is a sad day for us as our daughter Madge died at 3 this morning.* The next day he added these words to his journal . . . "*Oh my heart . . . how it aches for my dear daughter*".

For the first time in his twenty-year recording of matter-of-fact daily happenings, he wrote emotionally, revealing the depth of his grief at the death of the daughter who had been born in the log blockhouse, Fort Decatur.

In the seven years from 1888 to 1895 David and Louisa Denny suffered more tragedy than most families experience in a lifetime. Two of their children were taken by death. The beautiful home on Queen Anne Hill and the farm on the swale . . . even the site of the little log cabin above the bay . . . were gone, along with all the enterprises David Denny and his sons had founded. Almost overnight the man who was said to be one of Seattle wealthiest citizens became one of its poorest. With the loss of fortune and the attack on his good name, came the loss of most of those who had claimed to be his friends.

The so-called "Deficiency Judgment" authorized by the laws of that time permitted creditors to take over all the assets of the debtor, with no provision for the return of any surplus that might be left after the property was disposed of and the debt liquidated.

Of the stunning financial disaster that befell her father, Emily Inez Denny wrote:

"*The failure of Baring Bros., (an international London banking house) as he told me repeatedly, began it . . . theirs being the result of having taken bonds of the Argentine Republic, and a revolution happening along, $100,000,000.00 went by the board; a sizeable failure.*

"*Partly on acount of this and partly on account of the vast advantage of the lender over the borrower, and partly through the vast anxiety of those who held his securities, they were able to distribute among themselves his hard-earned fortune.*

"*The Deficiency Judgment also loomed large and frequent and his last days were disturbed by those who still pressed their greedy claims, even following after his death, with a false, unjust and monstrous sale of the cemetery in which he lies buried!*

"*The Deficiency Judgment and renewal of the same gives opportunity for greedy and unprincipled creditors to rob the debtor. There should be a law compelling the return of the surplus. When one class of people make many times their money out of the misfortunes of others, there is manifestly great inequality. The principles of some are to grab all they can, 'skin' all they can, and follow up all they can even to the graveyard*".

The stalwart young pioneer, David Denny, had arrived at "Smaquamox" in 1851 with twenty-five cents in his pocket. By the end of the three years of litigation and foreclosures that followed the crash of 1893, he was left with less than that. And he was no longer young. By the time the last scraps of his estate were gobbled up by lawyers, creditors and courts, he was approaching the age of sixty-five.

Furthermore, Seattle was a far different place in 1895 than it had been in the 1850's. It was no longer a close-knit village of friends and neighbors, who shared what they had in times of want, but a city with a growing financial district as its heart.

This fact was brought home bitterly to David Denny when the banking firm of Dexter Horton & Company, of which his brother Arthur was the senior vice president, joined the other creditors to force his bankruptcy.

The fine home, "Decatur Terrace," which David had built for Louisa and the family on Queen Anne, was among the last of their possessions to be foreclosed and it was there, on January 23, 1895, that David and Louisa observed their forty-second wedding anniversary . . . and the anniversary of the first wedding in Seattle. The Seattle *Post-Intelligencer* reported the event in glowing terms, ignoring the fact that its principles were about to be evicted from their "present beautiful residence":

"*One of the notable features of the evening*", the *Post-Intelligencer* reported, "*was the large gathering of pioneers who col-*

lectively represented more years of residence in Seattle than ever were found together before.

"What added interest to the occasion was the historical fact that Mr. and Mrs. Denny were the first couple married in Seattle, and the transformation from the small, uncouth log cabin, built forty-three years ago by the sturdy young pioneer for his bride, to the present beautiful residence with all its modern conveniences in which the respected couple are enjoying the fruits of a well spent life".

Apparently filled with nostalgia and unaware of the irony of what he had written, the reporter continued:

"All present were more or less connected with the history of Seattle, all knew one another's history, and with their children and grandchildren the gathering, unconventional in every respect, with the two-year-old baby romping in the arms of the octogenarian, presented a colossal, happy family reunion.

"The old pioneer days were not forgotten, and one corner of the reception room was made to represent the interior of a cabin, lined with newspapers, decorated with gun, bullet pouch and powder horn and measure, a calico sunbonnet, a straw hat and hunting shirt.

"A table was set to represent one of the early fifties, namely, two boards across two boxes, for a table, a smoked salmon, a tin plate full of boiled potatoes, some sea biscuits and a few large clams. Such a meal, when it was had, was supposed to be a feast.

"Many other relics were in sight: a thirty-two pound solid shot, fired by the sloop-of-war Decatur among the Indians during the uprising; a ten-pound shot belonging to Dr. Maynard's cannon; a pair of enormous elk's horns belonging to a six hundred and thirty-pound elk killed by Mr. D.T. Denny, September 7, 1869, in the woods north of Green Lake; the first Bible of the family from which the eldest daughter, Miss Emily Inez, learned her letters; an old-fashioned Indian halibut hook, an ingenious contrivance; an old family Bible, once the property of the father of David T. Denny, bearing the following inscription on the inside cover:

" 'The property of J. Denny,
Purchased of J. Strange,
August the 15th, 1829,
Price 62½ cents.
Putnam County, Indiana'

"Also a number of daguerreotypes of Mr. and Mrs. D.T. Denny in the early years of their married life, taken in the fifties, and one of W.G. Latimer and his sister. All these and many more afforded food for conversations and reminiscences on the part of the old pioneers present.

"An informal programme introduced the social intercourse of the evening. Harold Denny, a grandson of the hosts and son of Mr. John B. Denny, made an address to his grandparents, giving them the greeting of the assembly in these words:

" 'O fortunate, O happy day,
The people sing, the people say,
The bride and bridegroom, pioneers,
Crowned now with good and gracious years
Serenely smile upon the scene.
The growing state they helped to found
Unto their praise shall yet redound.
Oh may they see a green old age,
With every leaf a written page
Of joy and peace from day to day.
In good, new times not far away
May people sing and people say,
'Heaven bless their coming years;
Honor the noble pioneers.'

"The chief diversion was afforded by the sudden entrance of a band of sixteen young men and women gorgeously dressed as Indians, preceded by a runner who announced their approach. They were headed by Capt. D.T. Davies who acted as chief. The band marched in true Indian file, formed a circle and sat down on the floor with their 'tamanuse' boards upon which they beat the old time music and sang their Indian songs. After an impressive hush, the chief addressed the white chief, Denny, in the Chinook language, wishing Mr. and Mrs. Denny many happy returns of the auspicious occasion.

"Mr. Denny, who is an adept in the Indian languages, replied in the same tongue, thanking his dark brethren for their good intentions and speaking of the happy relations that always existed between the whites and the Indians until bad white men and whiskey turned the minds and brains of the Indians. The council then broke up and took their departure.

"The marriage certificate of Mr. and Mrs. Denny is written on heavy blue paper and has been so carefully preserved that, beyond the slight fading of the ink, it is as perfect as when *first given in the dense forests on the shores of Elliott Bay. It reads as follows:*

" 'This may certify that David Denny and Louisa Boren were joined in marriage at the residence of Arthur A. Denny in the County of King and Territory of Oregon, by me in the presence of A.A. Denny and wife and others, on this 23rd day of January, 1853. D.S. Maynard, J.P.'

"Mr. and Mrs. David T. Denny have had eight children, four daughters and four sons. One son died shortly after birth, and all the others grew to maturity, after which the father and mother were called to mourn the loss of two daughters. Two daughters and three sons survive, namely: Miss Emily Inez, Mrs. Abbie D. Lindsley, Mr. John B. Denny, Mr. D. Thomas Denny and Mr. Victor W.S. Denny.

"The sons are all married and nine out of ten grandchildren were present last evening to gladden the hearts of Grandpa and Grandma Denny. The absent members of the family group were Mrs. John B. Denny and daughter, in New York on a visit.

" 'People in these days of modern improvements and plenty know nothing of the hardships the pioneer of forty years ago had to undergo right here,' said Mr. Denny.

" 'Nearly forty years of life in a dense forest surrounded by savages and wild beasts, with the hardest kind of work necessary in order to eke out an existence, was the lot of every man and woman here. It was a life of privation, inconveniences, anxieties, fears and dangers innumerable, and required physical and mental strength to live it out. Of course, we all had good health, for in twenty-four year's time we only had a doctor four times. Our colony grew little by little, good men and bad men came in and by the time the Indians wanted to massacre us we had about three hundred men, women and children. We got our provisions from ships that took our piles and then the Indians also furnished us with venison, potatoes, fish, clams and wild fowl. Flour, sugar and coffee we got from San Francisco. When we could get no flour, we made a shift to live on potatoes'.

"*The unique invitations sent out for this anniversary, consisted of a fringed piece of buckskin stretched over the card and painted '1851, Ankuti. 1895, Okoke Sun.'** They were well responded to, and every room in the large house was filled with interested guests, from the baby in arms to the white haired friend of the old people. Pioneers were plenty, and it is doubtful if there ever was a gathering in the City of Seattle that could aggregate so many years of residence in the Queen City of the West on the shores of Elliott Bay.

"Arranged according to families, and classing those as pioneers who came prior to the Indian war of 1855 - 56, the following list will be found of historical value:

"Rev. and Mrs. D.E. Blaine, pioneers; A.A. Denny, brother of D.T. Denny; Loretta Denny, sister of D.T. Denny; Lenora Denny, daughter of A.A. Denny; Rev. and Mrs. Daniel Bagley; pioneers of 1852, Oregon, Seattle 1860; Mrs. Clarence B. Bagley, daughter of Thomas Mercer, 1852; C.B. Bagley, pioneer, 1852 Oregon, Seattle 1860; Hillory Butler, pioneer; Mrs. Gardner Kellogg, daughter of Bonney, Pierce County 1853; Walter Graham, pioneer; Rev. Geo. F. Whitworth, pioneer; Thomas Mercer, 1852 Oregon, Seattle 1853; David Graham, 1858; Mrs. Susan Graham, daughter of Thomas Mercer; Mrs. S.D. Libby, wife of Captain Libby, pioneer; George Frye, 1853; Mrs. Katherine Frye, daughter of A.A. Denny; Sophie and Bertie Frye, granddaughters of A.A. Denny; Mrs. Mamie Kauffman Dawson, granddaughter of Wm. N. Bell, pioneer; Mr. and Mrs. D.B. Ward, pioneers (Mrs. Ward, daughter of Charles Byles, of Thurston County, 1853); Mrs. Abbie D. Lindsley, daughter of D.T. and Louisa Denny; the Bryans, all children of Edgar Bryan, a pioneer of Thurston County; J.W. George, pioneer 1852; Orange Jacobs, pioneer of Oregon".

This was the last time that the wagon train pioneers of the 1850's would gather together at the home of David and Louisa Denny.

---

[a]Since most Seattleites of 1895 were familiar with the Chinook jargon, the *Post-Intelligencer* didn't bother to translate the words "Ankuti", meaning "Long Ago", and "Okoke Sun", meaning "Today".

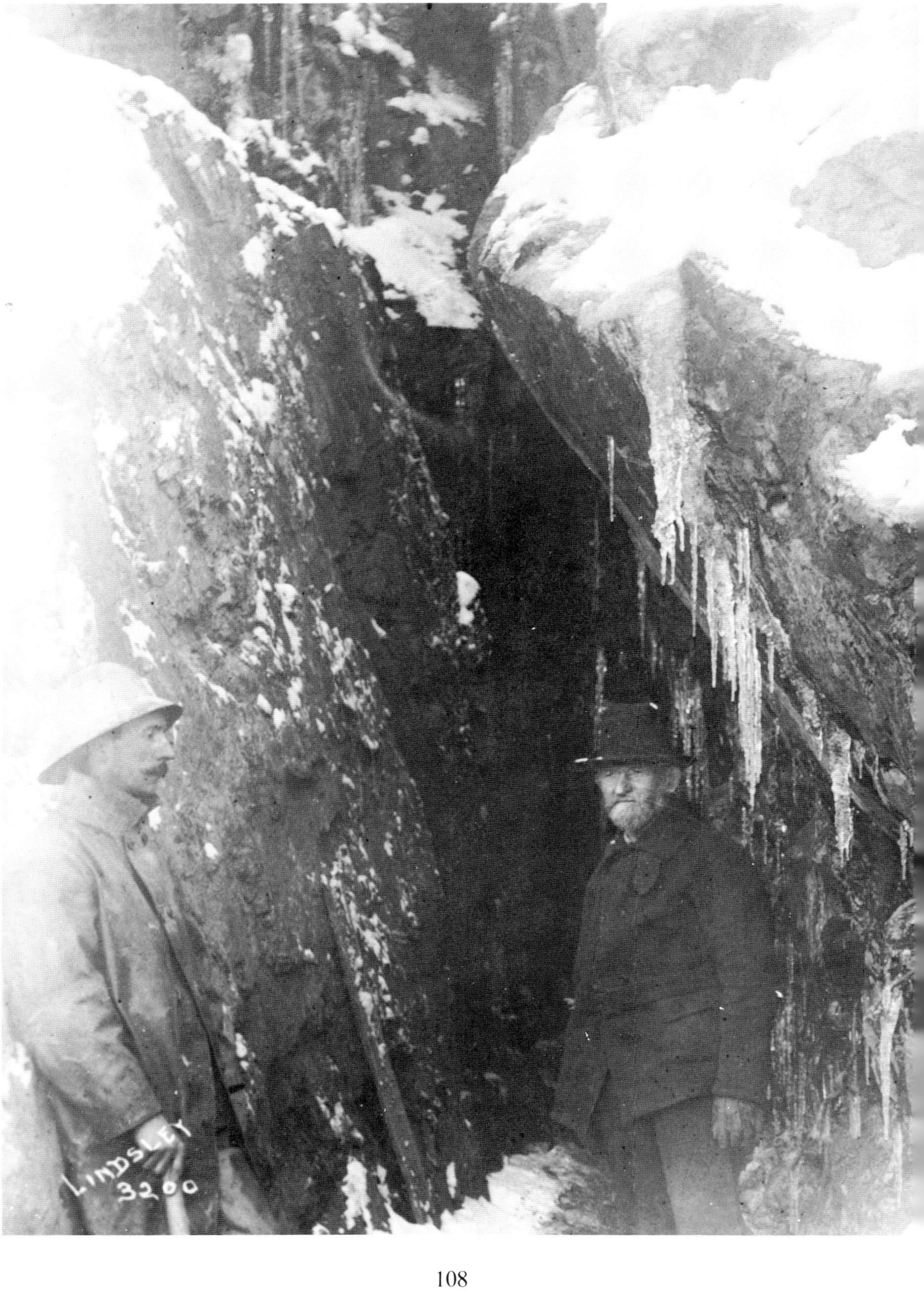
LINDSLEY
3200

EPILOGUE

Return to the Wilderness

In the end, the young pioneer who had waited alone in the wilderness of Smaquamox for the arrival of his beloved, returned with her to the peace and solitude of the forest.

For a time after the mansion on Queen Anne was taken from them, David and Louisa lived in a small house near the northern edge of their old claim at Fremont, but the holders of the Deficiency Judgments soon claimed that too. All that was left was a place at the family's old wilderness retreat at Licton Springs, which he had given to his daughter Emily in happier days.

There, in a tiny cottage not much larger than the original honeymoon cabin of 1853, David Denny lived out his few remaining years with the only woman he had ever loved, Louisa Boren.

It was when he left his last home at Fremont that Seattle's first citizen spoke his only recorded words of bitterness.

According to Roberta Frye Watt, "When he left his city home for the last time, he said as he paused at the door, and sadly looked about, 'I'll never look upon Seattle again.' Then, like a sorrowing father turning his back upon an ungrateful child, he went out of the city to his humble home in the woods. The forest had given him shelter when he first came, the forest sheltered him and his wounded heart in the end".

"Yet", she added, "I cannot write David's life as having had an unhappy ending. A life so well spent, so tenderly cherished by loved ones, and a name written so generously into the history of Seattle, a name that has come down to the city of today as a synonym of all that is upright and honest, are greater than wealth".

Certainly David Denny didn't spend his later years feeling sorry for himself. Instead he started over again, prospecting for gold in the High Cascades. The Esther, Louisa and Ivanhoe claims on the headwaters of Gold Creek were profitable for a few years until the vein "petered out" and his son Victor, then a skilled mining engineer and assayist, worked with him, driving pack trains from Licton Springs to the mountain mines and over dangerous trails from Gold Creek to Easton, the horses laden with gold ore to be shipped over the mountains by rail.

In 1899, at the age of sixty-seven, he was given a contract to make improvements on the Snoqualmie Pass road across the Cascade Mountains. In a detailed report to the King County commissioners, he wrote that, "I began work on the third day of June, 1899, and closed on the 23rd day of September. I made 412 feet of bridges and put down over 1200 feet of corduroy, made 3040 feet of new road and removed a large amount of rock from the road, nearly 200 blasts".

Opposite page: Victor W. S. and David Denny at the entrance to the Esther Mine in the Cascade Mountains.

David Denny at his mining cabin in the high Cascades.

Opposite page: Stock certificate in Esther Gold and Silver Mining Company, issued to Emily Inez Denny in 1900.

INCORPORATED UNDER THE LAWS OF THE STATE OF WASHINGTON

Shares 125

No 86

Esther Gold and Silver Mining Company

OF SEATTLE, WASHINGTON

Capital Stock $1,500,000

THIS CERTIFIES THAT E. Inez Denny is the owner of One Hundred & twenty five Shares of the Capital Stock of **Esther Gold and Silver Mining Company** FULLY PAID AND NON-ASSESSABLE transferable only on the Books of the Corporation in person or by Attorney on surrender of this Certificate

In Witness Whereof, the duly authorized officers of this Corporation have hereunto subscribed their names and caused the corporate Seal to be hereto affixed at Seattle, Wash. this sixteenth day of October A.D. 1906

Victor M Denny, SECRETARY

D. T. Denny, PRESIDENT

$1.00 EACH SHARES

NOTICE OF LOCATION
—OF THE—

Silver Bell Lode Claim; Discovered _____ 1896 _____ 190___, Located _Oct 17_ 190___

Notice is hereby given that the undersigned, having complied with the mining act of Congress, approved May 10, 1872, and with all subsequent acts, and with local laws, customs and regulations, ha__s__ this _____ day of _Oct 1896_ 190___, located and claimed _1500_ linear feet and horizontal measurement on the _Silver Bell_ lode, vein, ledge, or deposit, along the vein thereof, with all its dips, spurs, angles and variations, as allowed by law, together with 300 feet on each side of the middle of said vein at surface ground within the lines of said claim, which is situated in _Gold Creek_ Mining District, County of _Kittitas_, State of Washington, and is described by metes and bounds as follows. Commencing at _Discovery thence south 750 ft thence east 300 ft, thence south 1500 ft, thence west 600 ft, thence south 1500 ft, thence east 300 ft._

Witness: Located by

Lowman & Hanford Stationery and Printing Company's Blank No. 199—LOCATION NOTICE—SHORT FORM.

Opposite page: In addition to his other duties, Victor W. S. Denny, shown here with Lawrence Lindsley, provided game for the mine cookhouse.

Left: Mine location notice, signed by Louisa Denny and witnessed by her husband and son.

Above: Victor W. S. Denny and a part of the mine crew at the cookhouse, 1889.

The rugged old pioneer worked with the road crew, camping along the way and personally supervising the construction and blasting. When a careless worker swung a double-bitted ax and struck him between the eyes, he wrapped a bandage around his head until the bleeding stopped and went back to work. During September the pass was soaked with a continuous deluge of rain, which, according to the report *"made it impossible to keep the powder dry"*.

David Denny, approaching his Biblical allotment of three score years and ten, was living as he had at Smaquamox in 1851, working and sleeping in rain-soaked clothing and soggy blankets and suffering from an untended ax wound.

But then he had been nineteen years old and there had seemed no limit to his vitality and endurance. Now the malicious years had caught up with him at last and the limit had been reached.

During the summer of 1900 he returned to the Cascades for the last time, camping at Lake Keechelus, just east of the Snoqualmie Pass, in the interests of a mining company. He was able to enjoy some fishing and prospecting and even a bit of hunting in this last Indian Summer of his life.

After that, according to his daughter, *"Gradually some maladies which had haunted him for years increased. As long as he could he exerted himself in helping his family, especially in preparing the site for a new home. He soon after became a great sufferer for several years, struggling against his infirmities, in all exhibiting great fortitude and patience"*.

On the evening of November 25, 1903 . . . forty-eight years and twelve days after the

Assay report of Denny Brothers, 1907.

The David Denny family's summer cabin near Licton Springs.

landing of the pioneers at Smaquamox... the lead story of the Seattle *Times* began:

"David Thomas Denny, one of the founders of Seattle, died at 3:36 o'clock this morning at his residence at Licton Park, near Green Lake".

The Seattle papers were filled with eulogies of prominent citizens, including a number who had participated in the financial ruin of David Denny. That of his longtime pastor, the Reverend W.S. Harrington, provided one of the most perceptive insights of his true character... *"He was retiring and his strength was known to few... He believed in a religion which he sought to live, not to exhibit".*

Because he was retiring and his strength cloaked in gentleness, much of the stirring part he played in the founding and building of Seattle has been forgotten.

Yet it was David Denny who guided and guarded the little wagon train from Cherry

Pack horse trail to the Denny mine.

Grove and led the successful defense against the hostile Indians while most of the party lay sick and helpless in a wagon bed.

It was David Denny who walked the wilderness trail from the Willamette to Puget Sound and chose Elliott Bay as the site for the party's final stopping place.

It was David Denny who led the volunteer patrol into the Indian ambush on the White River to search for survivors of Lieutenant Slaughter's defeated regulars and guarded the door of Fort Decatur during the Indian attack on Seattle.

And it was David Denny who, more than any other man, gave his own resources to build Seattle from a sawmill village to a major city.

And because he "believed in a religion that he sought to live, not to exhibit", he emerges from the dusty pages of history as a

Louisa Denny in her later years, with her grandson.

The Daily Times

DAILY SOCIETY NEWS
In the Daily
Women's Department
See Page 16

WEDNESDAY EVENING, NOV. 25, 1903.   FIVE CENTS EVERYWHERE

ORTED SUNK IN COLLISION
T B. F. DAY IS DISMISSED
MITER BOUND FOR SEATTLE
DEAD AFTER LONG ILLNESS
OF SEATTLE START REVOLT

ICAGO STRIKERS RETURN TO WORK

ployes Agree to Submit the Question of Wages to Arbitration.

ms of Peace Do Not Require the Company to Recognize the Union.

Last of Seattle's Early Settlers Passes Away

DAVID T. DENNY IS DEAD

Seattle's Oldest Pioneer Passes Away at Licton Park.

Sketch of the Life of a Very Remarkable Man.

DAVID THOMAS DENNY, one of the founders of Seattle, died at 2:26 o'clock this morning at his residence at Licton Park, near Green Lake. His wife and all of his children, one cousin and several of his grandchildren were at the bedside at the end, as was the Rev. B. Benjamin, pastor of the Green Lake M. E. Church.

Mr. Denny's end was peaceful and without pain. He lapsed into his last unconsciousness about half an hour before his final dissolution. During the night he suffered a great deal and almost his last audible words were to be lifted so that the pain might be eased somewhat. The expression "Oh, Lord, help me!" came frequently to his lips during those distressing moments.

The funeral will take place on Sunday afternoon at 1 o'clock at the First M. E. Church, at the corner of Third Avenue and Marion Street. The body will be brought in to the embalming rooms of Butterworth & Sons tomorrow morning at 10 o'clock, and in all probability will lie in state at the undertaking parlors on Saturday afternoon, that the remains may be viewed by such of his immediate and old-time friends as are unable to attend the Sunday service. At the church services the Rev. W. A. Harrington will officiate. Interment will be in the family lot at Oak Lake Cemetery, Green Lake. There will be both honorary and active pall-bearers, but the selection has not as yet been made.

The announcement of Mr. Denny's death this morning brought a flood of memories and deep sadness to many of his long-time friends. Tears showed in many eyes when these friends heard from a reporter for The Times, for the first time, of the final end. Probably the most expressive and fitting of all the comments heard upon the character and life of Mr. Denny was made by Mr. Dexter Horton, as follows:

Dexter Horton's Tribute.

"I have known Mr. Denny for fifty years. A mighty tree has fallen. He was one of the best men, of highest character and principle this city ever claimed as a citizen. That is enough."

By Father F. X. Prefontaine of the Church of Our Lady of Good Help: "I have known Mr. Denny about thirty-six or thirty-seven years. I always liked him, though I was more intimately acquainted with his brother, Hon. A. A. Denny, and his venerable father, John

(Continued on Page Three.)

Seattle Daily Times *report on the death of David Denny.*

116

warm and very likeable human being. A man of whom a pioneer friend of nearly half a century, Samuel Coombs, said:

"Of David Denny it may be said that if others had applied the Golden Rule as he did, he would have been living in his old home in great comfort in this city today".

In the archives of Seattle's Museum of History and Industry is a two-page document hand-written by David Denny on the ornate letterhead of David Denny & Son, which was drawn and lettered by his daughter Emily Inez. It is dated April 30, 1896, after the last of his wealth and property had been taken from him, and is addressed to no one in particular.

In it the old frontiersman, whose writings had generally been limited to workaday journal entries of timber cut, crops harvested and books read, outlined his own appraisal of his life and his religious philosophy. He had come to the conclusion that sectarian religion wasn't important . . . that *"there are many good Christians in each and all churches"*; that, in fact, it was *"not absolutely essential to belong to any church"* in order to practice the basic concepts of Christianity.

Perhaps he was remembering hard-drinking Doc Maynard, who had spent his life giving to others while his church-going contemporaries were busy taking. In any event, it is solid evidence that his innate spirit of tolerance was stronger than a lifetime of narrow nineteenth century religious doctrine.

Even more revealing is his own summary of his life and what aspects of it he considered important enough to put down in writing for those who would come after him. He makes no mention of the fortune he lost; only of the things that had been basics to him since the beginning:

"In looking back over my pioneer life I can see many places where I would do differently had I the chance to pass that way again, but knowing what I do now, I would come to Puget Sound to Elliott Bay and locate just as I did before except that I would make my home on the waterfront. I would marry the same woman, join the same church, but endeavor to be a better Christian".

Louisa Boren Denny, the fairytale "sweetbriar bride" of Seattle's first romance, was almost ninety when she passed quietly away on August 18, 1916. The pioneer woman who had chopped the logs for the foundation of the first building in what was to become downtown Seattle, had lived to see that city grow to a metropolis of 300,000, its rising skyline dominated by a forty-two story office building on Carson Boren's old claim where she had cut down the fir trees in the wilderness.

But, like David, Louisa was less concerned with rising skyline and population figures than with the natural beauties of the green and lovely land that had been her adopted home for sixty-five years . . . the stately forests, the wind-swept beaches and the ever-changing reaches of the Inland Sea.

"In the last summer of Louisa's life", it was written, *"she asked to be taken where she could see the water and hear the waves on the beach. There in a little cottage facing west, within sound of the lapping waters of Puget Sound, she passed on to meet David on the other shore"*.

D. T. DENNY & SONS. No 124
REAL ESTATE BROKERS. Harrison St.

DEALINGS FAIR
PRICES REASONABLE.

SEATTLE
ET MEA MESSISIS ERIT.

Seattle, Wash., Apr 30 1896

In looking back over my Pioneer life I can see many places where I would do differently had I the chance to pass that way again, but knowing what I do now I would had I chance I would come to Puget Sound to Elliot Bay and locate just as I did before except that I would make my home on the waterfront. I would marry the same woman — join the same church but endeavor to be a better Christian. I can safely say that my experience has not made a Spectaman light of me. I most fully believe there are many good Christians in each and all of the Churches — in fact that it is not absolutely essential to belong to any church and yet it is much

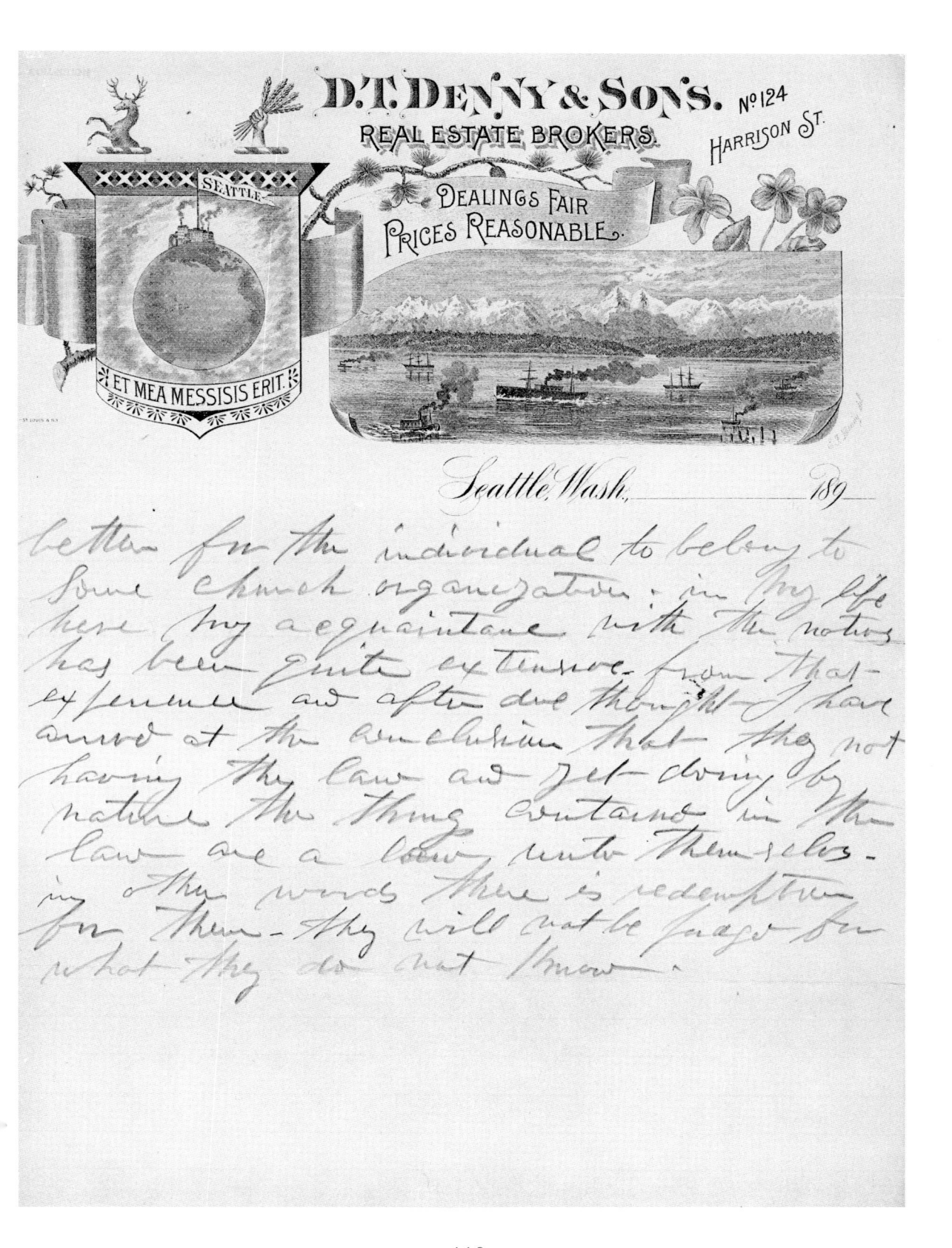

D. T. DENNY & SONS. № 124
REAL ESTATE BROKERS HARRISON ST.

SEATTLE
ET MEA MESSISIS ERIT.

DEALINGS FAIR
PRICES REASONABLE

Seattle, Wash., _____ 189__

better for the individual to belong to some church organization. In my life here my acquaintance with the notion has been quite extensive. From that experience and after due thought I have arrived at the conclusion that they not having the law and yet doing by nature the things contained in the law are a law unto themselves — in other words there is redemption for them — they will not be judged for what they do not know.

The Felker House—Seattle's first hotel.

Victor W. S. Denny at Ptarmigan Park, head of Gold Creek, Lake Keechelus, about 1895.

The log cookhouse, Yesler Mill

INDEX

Active, USS 78, 82
Alexander, John 35
Alexander, Frances 34-37, 40, 42
Alexander, John S. 35
Andrews, L. B. 11-12
Applegate, Jesse 22
Applegate, Lindsay 22
Armstrong, John 9

Bachelder, Charles 43
Bagley, C. B. 13, 107
Bagley, Mrs. C. B. 107
Bagley, Rev. Daniel 68, 94-95, 107
Beaver, steamship 43
Bell, Sarah 34, 41, 63
Bell, Virginia 79
Bell, William 34, 45-46, 49, 55, 63, 66, 95, 107
Blaine, Catherine 56, 70, 79, 81-82, 86, 107
Blaine, Rev. David E. 56, 58, 67, 70, 82, 107
Boren, Carson 16-19, 23, 26, 45-46, 49-51
     55, 63-66, 71, 80, 95, 117
Boren, Mrs. Carson 50-51
Boren, Gertrude 26
Boren, William R. 88, 96
Brannon, W. H. 75
Bryan, Edgar 107
Butler, Hillory 71, 77, 79, 107
Byles, Charles 107

Chenowith, F. A. 26-27
Cherry, Dr. W. G. 67
Clark, E. A. 66
Clark, Frank 69
Collins, Lucinda 31
Collins, Luther 31-33, 65-66, 68
Conklin, Mary Ann 56, 69
Coombs, Samuel 117

D. T. Denny & Son 96, 99, 117-119
Davies, Capt. D. T. 106
Dawson, Mamie K. 107

Decatur, USS 72-80, 82, 106
Denny, A. W. 11, 16
Denny, Abbie Lena 85
Denny, Anna Louise 85, 104
Denny, Alford 11, 16
Denny, Arthur A. 11-17, 20, 23-27, 33-36, 40-43
     46, 49-60, 65-68, 70, 73, 75, 82, 84, 94, 97, 104-105, 107
Denny, David, Sr. 6, 8-9, 13
Denny, David T. 1, 5-6, 11, 16, 19, 21-25, 28-33
     37-45, 49-59, 63, 65, 68, 70-86, 88-99, 103-109, 112,
     114-115, 117
Denny, David T., Jr. 85, 89-90, 98, 104, 107
Denny, Emily Inez 13, 21, 51, 61, 63-64, 67, 79-80
     82, 84-86, 88-91, 99, 103, 105-107, 109, 117
Denny, Geoffrey 6
Denny, Harold 106
Denny, James 11, 16, 22
Denny, John 11-13, 16-18, 23, 34, 49, 53, 90, 94-95, 106
Denny, John B. 85, 90, 96, 104-107
Denny, John F. 11, 16
Denny, Lewis 11, 16
Denny, Lenora 107
Denny, Louisa 1, 14-17, 21-28, 37, 40, 44-45, 49-52
     57-67, 70-71, 74, 77-85, 88, 90, 93-99, 104-109, 117
Denny, Loretta 16, 53, 107
Denny, Madge Decatur 81, 104-105
Denny, Margaret 9
Denny, Margaret L. 16, 26
Denny, Mary B. 15-16, 20, 25-27, 40-41, 45-46, 50
     55-56
Denny, Rachel 10
Denny, Robert, 9-10 9-10
Denny, Samuel 9
Denny, Samuel (2) 11, 16
Denny, Sarah 11
Denny, Sarah Boren 12, 14, 23, 25, 34, 53-54
Denny, Sarah W. 11, 12
Denny, Victor W. S. 85, 89-90, 104
Denny, Victor W. S., Jr. 1, 78
Denny, Walter 10
Denny, William H. 6

121

Denny, William & Bros. 6
Dexter Horton & Co. 97, 105
Dixon, Margaret C. Denny 6
Drew, John 77
Dunlap, Edmund 14
Dunlap, Pamelia 14, 61

Elliott, J. L. 4
Evans, Elwood 69
Exact, schooner 33-38, 49

Fay, Capt. Robert C. 28, 30-32, 34-35, 37
Felker, Capt. L. M. 52, 56
Felker House 56, 67, 69, 79, 81
Folger, Capt. Isaiah 33, 36-38, 49
Fort Decatur 77-78, 81
Franklin Adams, brig 52-53, 56
Frye, George 107
Frye, Katherine 107
Frye, Sophie 107

Gansevoort, Capt. Guert 77-80, 82
George, J. W. 107
Graham, David 80
Graham, Susan 107
Graham, Walter 107
Grant, Frederic 50
Great Northern Railway 53
Griffith, L. H. 99

Hanford, C. H. 50
Harrington, Rev. W. S. 114
Hastings, L. B. 42
Heebner, William 68-69
Henry, brig 27
Hewitt, Christopher C. 72, 75-76
Holgate, Milton 77, 79
Horton, Dexter 68, 99
Horton, Denny & Phillips 68
Howard, Capt. Daniel 43
Hubbard, Isabella Denny 8
Hudson's Bay Company 4, 22, 43

Jacobs, Judge Orange 107
James P. Flint, steamboat 27
John Davis, brig 52

Kellogg, Mrs. Gardner 107
King, John 74
Kirkland, Moses 79
Krug, Adolph 99, 102-103

Lander, Judge Edward 55, 71
Latimer, W. G. 53-54
Leonesa, brig 43-44, 46, 72
Leschi 70, 77, 80-81
Libby, Capt. S. D. 107
Libby, Mrs. S. D. 107
Lincoln, Abraham 12, 72, 94-95
Low, John N. 23-28, 30-33, 37, 41-43, 55, 95
Low, Lydia 34

McConaha, Eugenia 53, 60, 77, 79
McConaha, George 53, 60
McCurdy, H. W. 1
Maple, E. B. 53
Maple, Jacob 31, 32
Maple, Samuel 31, 45
Mason, Charles 70, 73
Massachusetts, USS 82

Maurer, David 56, 68-69
Maynard, Dr. David 49-57, 59-61, 65-66, 68, 74
                                82, 89, 95, 107, 117
Meeker, Ezra 48, 78
Mercer, Thomas 56-57, 68, 80, 85-86, 107
Mesachie Jim 65, 67
Moxlie's Canoe Express 56

Nollop, Charles 90
Northern Pacific Railway 95

Olympia Columbian 46, 48, 52, 56
Olympia Pioneer & Democrat 70

Pepper, Tom 78
Pettygrove, F. W. 42
Phelps, Lt. Thomas 74-75, 78
Phillips, David 68
Pierce, Farley 12
Plummer, Alfred 43
Plummer, Capt. George 52
Porter, Allen L. 71, 73
Prosch, Thomas 68
Puyallup Tom 76

Quiemuth 70

Raber, Joe 90
Rainier Power & Railway Co. 98
Renton, Capt. William 56, 67
Russell, Thomas 67

Salmon Bay Curley 66, 74
Seattle, Chief 1-4, 30, 42, 49, 51-52, 65, 74
Seattle Daily Times 41, 95, 114
Seattle Electric Rwy. & Power 45, 54, 105
Seattle Post-Intelligencer 45, 54, 105
Shaw, George C. 67
Slaughter, Lt. W. A. 75-76
Smith, Dr. Henry A. 52-53
Speidel, William C. 16, 57
Sterrett, Capt. Isaac S. 72-74, 77
Stevens, Gov. Isaac I. 67, 69-70, 73, 77-78

Tecumseh, Chief 11, 78
Terry, Charles 28, 35-36, 42-49, 51, 55-56, 68-69
                                        82, 92, 95
Terry, Lee 28, 30-33, 41-42, 44, 51, 55, 95
Tolmie, Dr. William 4
Traveler, steamboat 75

University of Washington 91-95
Union Water Co. 97

Wallace, Liberty 12
Wallace, Capt. William 76
Ward, Mr. & Mrs. D. B. 107
Washington, George 8
Washington Improvement Co. 97
Water Lily, steamboat 70, 77
Watt, Roberta Frye 12, 14, 21, 33, 40, 50, 52, 56-57
                                59, 72, 82, 109
Webster, Capt. William 70, 77
Western Mill Co. 97
Wilkes, Lt. Charles 4, 46
Wilson, Robert 79

Yarkekman Jim 74, 78
Yelser, Henry L. 54-57, 59, 65, 78, 86, 99
Young, William 67